Praise for the Work of Dr. David James

Dr. David James has given us a book that is both a good read and a roadmap to fulfilling our dreams. As a master clinician and communicator, David teaches how to tap the unused power of our minds to achieve heath, abundance, success, and a happy life. I hope you enjoy reading this book as much as I did and that you let its words change your life.

—Joe Tabbanella
Hypnotherapist and instructor at the Hypnosis Motivation Institute

I'm a single mom trying my hardest to make it on my own in Los Angeles and improve life for my son and me. When I met Dr. David James, I felt broken on the inside, financially stuck, and in need of a serious faith lift. Within four months of working with him on a weekly basis, I was promoted at work with a 56 percent raise, landing a dream job in the engineering department that gives me an extra $20,000 a year doing what I love and solid confidence in myself to take on any obstacle that comes my way. My gratitude for Dr. David can't be quantified, and his work speaks for itself. I will undoubtedly be working with him for many, many years to come.

—Aletia Little
Computer programmer and student of Quantum Computing

I doubt I would have consulted a hypnotist. But I was attracted to David's fascinating background, his path from police sergeant to Episcopal priest to a focus on men and manhood (men's movement), to author, psychologist, and now hypnotherapy. This real-world credibility was certainly confirmed in working with David. He is down to earth, but effective.

—Laura Gottwald
Interior designer, New York City

Working with David has been extremely helpful, helping me gain perspective and strengthening my confidence. I never believed in hypnotherapy until our first session, but now I swear by it.

—*Jacob Kasher*
Songwriter

I have spent a lifetime trying to get my problems under control. A friend recommended Dr. David to me, and despite my reluctance, I met with him and discovered that he is a kind and powerful healer. Within just a few sessions, I uncovered the basis of many of my problems and now consider myself happier than I've ever been. This book reminds me of working with Dr. David because it shares so much of the good work he has done with me.

—*Cameron Black*
Attorney

Also by Dr. David James

What Are They Saying about Masculine Spirituality? Paulist Press, 1996

Sacred Vision: A Man's Journey, Author's Choice Press, 2000

Praise for *What Are They Saying About Masculine Spirituality?*

Books like this give me hope. Not only is it written by a man who is willing to "hang in there" and trust the Spirit, but David enthusiastically invites other men to join him in the great adventure that is the search for God.

—*Richard Rohr*
Author and the founder of the Center for Action and Contemplation

This delightful little book provides an excellent overview of how the men's movement has influenced developments in masculine spirituality. The author does a good job of fitting the main themes of the men's movement into a spirituality intentionally grounded in the symbols, stories, and reflections of men—one that is what he calls "a God-path that is dedicated to men and yet not ... anti-woman."

Jim Love, author and director of MENWEB

Praise for *Sacred Journey, A Man's Legacy*

David helps us—with doses of sanity, humanity, and confrontation—to recover the vision of our sacred role as responsible and joyful leaders in the human family.

—*Alan Jones*
Author and dean of Grace Cathedral in San Francisco

This book will surprise you—perhaps on every page. You will discover that he has blended wisdom from psychology, scripture, and life in every segment. You'll realize how sacred vision is created—from a soul's journey into deep things with the faith and wisdom of many voices.

—*Dwight Judy*
Author and Founder of the Oakwood Spiritual Life Institute

DISCOVERING YOUR
MAGNIFICENT MIND

FINDING FREEDOM, PROSPERITY AND HEALING

DR. DAVID JAMES

BALBOA.
PRESS

A DIVISION OF HAY HOUSE

Author Credits: Author of "What Are They Saying About Masculine Spirituality" and "Sacred Vision: A Man's Legacy

Balboa Press books may be ordered through booksellers or by contacting:

Balboa Press
A Division of Hay House
1663 Liberty Drive
Bloomington, IN 47403
www.balboapress.com
1 (877) 407-4847

Because of the dynamic nature of the Internet, any web addresses or links contained in this book may have changed since publication and may no longer be valid. The views expressed in this work are solely those of the author and do not necessarily reflect the views of the publisher, and the publisher hereby disclaims any responsibility for them.

The author of this book does not dispense medical advice or prescribe the use of any technique as a form of treatment for physical, emotional, or medical problems without the advice of a physician, either directly or indirectly. The intent of the author is only to offer information of a general nature to help you in your quest for emotional and spiritual well-being. In the event you use any of the information in this book for yourself, which is your constitutional right, the author and the publisher assume no responsibility for your actions.

Any people depicted in stock imagery provided by Thinkstock are models, and such images are being used for illustrative purposes only.
Certain stock imagery © Thinkstock.

Print information available on the last page.

ISBN: 978-1-5043-7464-4 (sc)
ISBN: 978-1-5043-7466-8 (hc)
ISBN: 978-1-5043-7465-1 (e)

Library of Congress Control Number: 2017902188

Balboa Press rev. date: 02/09/2017

To my daughters and their men,

Erin and Omar, Jessica and Luke,

and to my wonderful grandchildren,

Austin, Ava, Lola, Madison, Sara, and Wes.

May your live out the power of your magnificent
minds in the years to come and then pass it along to
your children and your children's children.

And to my beloved Jeannine. God saved the best for last.

CONTENTS

Water takes the shape of whatever container holds it, whether it be in a glass, a vase or a river bank. Likewise, your subconscious will create and manifest according to the images you habitually project upon it through your daily thinking. This is how your destiny is created. Your life is in your hands, to make of it what you choose.

—John Kehoe, author of *Mind Power into the 21ˢᵗ Century*

PREFACE

Human beings, by changing the inner attitudes of their minds,
can change the outer aspects of their lives.

—William James

L ucia (not her real name) sat in the back seat of my patrol car, handcuffed and sobbing. Ten minutes before, she had been trying to steal money from a vending machine in a Laundromat, hoping to grab some quick cash and get away. Responding to a crime-in-progress call, I walked through the front door and saw her with her arm wedged in the coin slot. Before I could get to Lucia, she broke free of the machine and bolted out the back door. And the chase, as they say, was on. She ran through a parking lot, over two fences, and finally into an abandoned building before I finally caught up with her. Offering no further resistance, she surrendered, and we walked back to the police car.

This was not Lucia's first brush with law enforcement. While not a career criminal, she had several arrests for theft and assault—all related to her addiction to opiates. In the back of my car, between her cries of anguish, she asked, "Why can't I stop? I'm ruining my life and the lives of my kids!" We talked a bit on the drive to the county jail, but it was clear to me that Lucia was in the grip of a power greater than she could deal with.

Fast-forward twenty years, and I am hearing confessions as an Episcopal priest in my parish church in Tracy, California. Having sensed a call to pursue my spiritual life more intentionally, I had retired from the police department, gone to seminary, and been ordained as a priest and put in charge of a congregation. Much like Roman Catholicism, the Episcopal Church has a full sacramental life that includes the practice of private confession if the parishioner so desires. So, as I participated in that sacrament with Michael (again, not his real name), I bore witness to something that he couldn't seem to let go of in relationships with his family. Try as he might, he felt trapped in codependency and found that he gave more of his time, talent, and treasure than even he thought was healthy. Much like Lucia twenty years before, his lament was, "Why can't I change? Am I always going to be stuck like this?"

In some ways, the question of change has haunted me all my adult life. Like everyone, I've had issues that just wouldn't seem to budge. Sometimes it was stubborn extra weight; at other times it was a vexing romantic relationship. I've ridden the roller coaster of financial abundance and lack more times that I care to count. I've had stunning professional success and humiliating personal defeats. But at the root of all my experiences was the desire to experience and maintain positive change in my life—and my inability to do so. Heaven knows I was good at short-term change; I could drop a quick fifteen pounds or run a 10K without too much problem, but the time came when a huge wall seemed to erect itself between me and what I had set out to accomplish in life.

My mother chalked it up to my "being lazy," regularly reminding me that I had "so much potential going to waste." Friends were slightly more sympathetic, but all thought I was searching for something deeper than what life was offering me at any given time.

For the past thirty years, I've been on a journey to understand how to make change that lasts. In addition to my college and seminary work, I received both masters and doctoral degrees in clinical psychology. First as a priest, then as a college professor, and finally in private practice, I worked with my clients as we explored change and all the ways that we resist it. And yet, as well versed as I was in the ways of cognitive psychology, I felt that there was something missing in the way we were going about making change.

After a particularly difficult period in both my personal and my professional life, I returned to Southern California and began a course of study in the power of the mind at the Hypnosis Motivation Institute in Tarzana, California. During that year of intensive training and clinical practice, I discovered fresh insights into the power of mind and saw firsthand how people experienced profound and powerful change in just a few sessions of hypnotherapy. I was amazed to discover that in those few sessions, the clients could make powerful and lasting change that often took months or years of traditional psychotherapy.

This both excited and disturbed me. How could it be, I wondered, that such knowledge and power was available and yet so few clinicians took advantage of it? I was to discover that part of the answer lies in the myths and misconceptions that surround the practice of hypnosis, thanks in large part to hypnotic stage shows. Often when people think of hypnosis, they think of the escapades of those performers who, seemingly under the control of the hypnotist, bark like dogs or begin to remove articles of clothing when triggered by a special word. These shows are fun escapes from everyday life, but they certainly don't approximate what happens in a certified hypnotherapist's office. While the stage hypnotist is about entertainment, the clinical hypnotherapist is dedicated to the process of transforming their clients' lives.

Another area that blocks the full embrace of hypnotherapy is our culture's medical model of change, which is highly materialistic. We've been trained from childhood to believe that if we are sick, we go to the doctor, who either gives us medicine or performs surgery on us. In other words, the body is very much like an automobile, and the physician is the mechanic. While many are beginning to embrace the mind-body connection in their medical practice (as we'll see in chapter 2), hypnosis is often seen as an alternative therapy lumped in with acupuncture, aromatherapy, and in some instances, even Chiropractic. The thinking goes that these therapies may work for some, but it's most likely only going to help a few "susceptible" or "weak-minded" people. Thus, the old paradigm of mechanical medicine often keeps people from trying modalities like hypnosis, which can truly change the course of their life.

Yet there is much emerging evidence coming out of universities around the world that hypnosis is a powerful agent for healing and transformation. In Europe, for example, brain surgery is now being done without anesthesia while the patient is in the hypnotic state. Closer to home, Harvard Medical School has proven that injuries heal faster when people have hypnotherapy in addition to traditional treatments, and dental procedures are regularly done across the country with the hypnotherapist sitting alongside the patient, leading him or her in a wonderful journey of relaxation and imagination.

The power of the mind is not limited to the medical arena. People have discovered that hypnosis is helpful in healing personal relationships, getting the job they've always wanted, or letting go of crippling habits and addictions. In the 1950s and '60s, Dr. Joseph Murphy regularly lectured to standing-room-only crowds in Los Angeles about the power of the mind to create the life of one's dreams. His genius was in applying biblical principles to the emerging mind-power movement, and upon his passing, thousands of people bore witness to the ways his teachings had changed their lives. But Dr. Murphy wasn't the only one to understand and apply these life-changing practices. In our day, people like Wayne Dyer, Deepak Chopra, Louise Hay, and Pam Grout have shown us how to access our deepest selves to make the powerful changes for which we yearn.

I've written this book to introduce you to the possibilities that await you as you learn to use your mind more effectively. In these pages, you'll learn more about how the mind works and how to access its power to make lasting change. We will discover the power of the mind to heal the body and see how pharmaceutical medicines could be a thing of your past. You will experience a new sense of purpose as you practice the exercises in this book and begin to experience hope that life is neither random nor out of control. Rather, you will see that you are the architect and creator of your life—and you always have been. Together we will embark on a journey of imagination and destiny, and you will have a greater sense of your personal power and purpose when we're done.

I now know the answer to the question Lucia asked me in the back of my police car and Michael asked in the confessional. Remember, both their version of the question "Why can't I stop?" If I could go back in time, it would be to let them both know that they were captive to their habits and addictions because they didn't know how to use the power of their mind to set themselves free. I now understand how to use the mind in a way that would have allowed my searching and yearning younger self to enjoy his life much sooner. I invite you to turn the page now, and let's begin the adventure into discovering your magnificent mind.

ACKNOWLEDGMENTS

E ach time I write a book, I want to acknowledge so many people because everyone I encounter is a teacher along my path. For those who have taught me through celebration as well adversity, thank you. I am at this place in my life today thanks to your presence in my life.

Specifically, thanks to the following:

My family, both biological and extended. Although I'm the papa now, I've learned so much about how to be in love with all of you.

Joe Tabbanella, hypnotherapist extraordinaire, actor, director, and friend. Our times together encourage me, and your eagle eye helped this book become all that it is.

Wally Conway and Ralph Rideout, my AA sponsors and friends who were a lifeline while I was learning to swim again.

Dr. James Buskirk, caring physician. You embody the archetype of the creative healer, and you helped me back on the path of life.

Rev. Jim Clarke, a stalwart and faithful friend of more than twenty years. We've worked together, hiked together, and dreamed together. You are a master of the inner world, and your insights and love have sustained me on my journey.

Jodi Nicholson, the "fabulous" coach whose encouragement launched this book project.

Men whom I've never met, yet who have been my teachers about the possibilities of the mind: Gregg Braden, Deepak Chopra, Joe Dispenza, Wayne Dyer, Neville Goddard, John Kappas, John Kehoe, Bruce Lipton, Joseph Murphy, and Paramahansa Yogananda. I trust that your work is reflected accurately in this book.

George Kappas and my colleagues at the Hypnosis Motivation Institute in Tarzana, California. You gave me the language to understand what my mind and heart already knew.

Dr. Rodney Collins and the dedicated group of healers at the New Visions Medical Group, where I am privileged to practice. You inspire me every day.

My clients, students, and conference participants. You taught me so much that I thought about giving you a refund.

INTRODUCTION

Imagination is the beginning of creation.
You imagine what you desire, you will what you
imagine, and at last you create what you will.

—George Bernard Shaw

C an you imagine your dream life? Would you be prosperous? Known for your generosity to people and causes important to you? Perhaps you'd be onstage accepting an Oscar or performing to a sold-out crowd at Carnegie Hall? Or you'd be free of a debilitating physical or emotional condition that has plagued you for years? Whatever your dream, it all begins in the workshop of your imagination. Everything that exists today, from the beauty of the Sistine Chapel to the reactor of a nuclear submarine, was first in the mind of its creator. We live in an age of such rapid expansion of technology that we forget that everything began as an idea in someone's imagination.

Napoleon Hill once said, "If you can conceive it, you can achieve it." So, let me ask you a question, why haven't your dreams come true? You may think it's because people or circumstances have blocked your advancement in life, or because your body has betrayed you, or because the government takes too much of your money in taxes. But the truth is that there is only one reason you're not at the level of happiness and success that you desire: *because you don't believe it's possible.* At some point, when your dream was in its infancy, a belief came along and killed it.

Your mind always responds to the stronger of two ideas, so your belief about lack and limitation, if it is stronger than your imagination, will kill your dream every time. Rather than face this truth head-on, we find something or someone to blame. But history is filled with stories of people who were undeterred by failure and went on to create wonders that benefit us all right now.

Napoleon Hill, called "America's resident philosopher-laureate of success and ethics," failed at business several times before he reached the pinnacle of achievement that he set for himself. And he didn't just fail to meet a deadline or two. He started a company and lost his fortune in the Great Depression; he founded a successful magazine only to have it stolen out from underneath him by unscrupulous business partners; he survived an assassination attempt; and he lost all the profits to his landmark book, *Think and Grow Rich*, in a nasty divorce. But none of these deterred him. As a young man, he imagined a life that was filled with goodness and success, and he never let anything get in the way of realizing that dream. He knew that the secret to creating a wondrous life dwelt in the storehouses of his mind.

Motivational books, workshops, and videos tell the stories of people who made their dreams come true despite daunting circumstances blocking them every step of the way. In one way or another, each story of accomplishment points to one fact: *belief won out over circumstance.* Many of us have heard of Sylvester Stallone's story of personal triumph over countless rejections and humiliation by Hollywood executives. We're spellbound when Michael Jordan tells us that he missed over nine thousand shots in his career, lost three hundred games, failed to make the game-winning shot twenty-six times, and yet went on to become one of the greatest basketball players ever. These stories and countless others like them serve as guideposts for you on your journey to fulfillment. By changing how and what you believe, you can change your life.

My primary purpose in writing this book is to help you change your beliefs and make your new beliefs allies, coaches, and cheerleaders as you launch your fantastic life. In other words, we'll see what's possible when your mind is working *for* you, and we'll learn how to access its untapped power to make powerful change that lasts.

With over thirty years in helping people connect with their deepest and truest self, I still get excited when I meet someone who is willing to do whatever it takes to change his or her life. I assume that since you're reading these words, you are one of the people who has chosen to thrive and experience all the goodness that Creative Intelligence (which some call God) has in store for you.

Spend five minutes browsing the shelves of your local bookstore or library, and you will see hundreds, if not thousands, of titles dedicated to self-empowerment and improvement. Some are masterpieces that contain real jewels of transformation tucked into hundreds of pages, waiting to be discovered by the serious reader.

Today we seem to be always on the go, so I've written this book to make the material easily accessible and available, with a recommended reading list at the end. Everything that I present here reflects the most up-to-date understanding of the journey of transformation, so you can dive into this material with me and find a way to make your dreams come true.

Chapter 1 of this work will introduce you to the power of your mind. We will begin our exploration of how the mind can bring powerful change to our bodies and the role of belief in all powerful change. We will begin to understand how the mind has two active processes, which we call the conscious and subconscious minds. In doing so, we will learn how we get the best results from our mind when we integrate and harmonize the activity of both. Then we will discover the relationship between our mind and our body and see that, as Dr. Candice Perth discovered, our body is the expression of our subconscious mind in many ways. Finally, in this chapter, you will be introduced to the ways that you can use your integrated mind to bring powerful changes to your relationships and finances.

Chapter 2 is a review of the power of the mind revealed in what is commonly called the placebo effect. Using stories and case studies, we will see how the mind is a primary driver in both disease and health, and we will discover that we already possess within ourselves a pharmacy of such healing power that, if properly harnessed, could reduce if not eliminate dependence on pills, shots, syrups, and inhalers altogether. We will also discover the power of negative words and thoughts and their impact on the body as well. The "nocebo" effect is in many ways as powerful as the placebo effect, and we will see examples of how authority figures have essentially doomed people to lives of disability through careless or harmful medical pronouncements.

In Chapter 3, we will dive into the mechanics of the magnificent mind. We will learn the operating system of our mind in-depth and see how the mind is essential in forming and maintaining either good or bad habits. In this chapter, we will begin to explore the role of the mind in both substance and process addictions and see how an integrated program of recovery should include proper mind management. The creative power of the mind is discussed here, and we will learn how to think both consciously and subconsciously to create a life that is rich and vivid in every sense of that word.

Chapter 4 reveals six principles of the subconscious mind that, when understood, allow to us to make dramatic and powerful change. We will examine the symbolic nature of the subconscious mind and see how it is always alert and ready to make the changes you desire. And this chapter will reveal how the subconscious mind integrates the material that comes from the conscious mind and allows us to go deeper than we ever imagined.

In Chapter 5, we will begin to experience practical ways to make the changes we desire. Beginning with understanding the power of our state of mind, we will see that literally what we think we become. We will delve into the mystery that is the process of homeostasis—that is the body-mind's automatic default setting that resists change. We will also look at what to do about correcting its well-meaning but misguided attempts to block our transformation.

In this chapter, you will experience a meditation that will unlock your body awareness and allow you to be open to the change process that's on its way. Finally, we will explore the fight-flight-freeze process and see how it impedes the changes we want to make in our lives by locking our nervous system into a pattern of rejection and rebellion.

By the time we arrive at chapter six, we will be ready for miracles. As we become more familiar with the landscape of the mind, we will examine and adopt three gifts that allow us to make change exponentially. First we will discover the power of clarity of and focus. Next we will look at the power of intention and experience a way to harness its power for growth. Then we will discover the power of release and see how to let go of energetic blocks and thought patterns that keep you from achieving the level of health and success that you desire. Finally, we will revisit the use of imagination in the process of creation and see how it is an actual function of the subconscious mind and will move us powerfully toward the people we want to be.

In the final chapter, we will begin the process of creating the "new you." Using story, symbol, metaphor, release, imagination, and the processes learned in this book, we will unleash the creative power within your integrated and powerful mind to see changes occur before your eyes. We will see personality and thinking patterns that are common to people who recover from life-threatening and debilitating diseases, and we will begin to explore the next step in your transformation: unfolding your connecting to your highest self in union with the Divine.

As you can see, we are going to undertake a lot in a few pages, but I guarantee that every bit of intention and attention that you dedicate to the work will bear rich and abundant fruit.

After a lifetime of service as well as training as a cognitive psychologist and spiritual director, I write this book from the point of view of a hypnotherapist and transformational agent. My positive bias is that the subconscious mind can be known and reprogrammed to make the change you desire. In my office and conferences, I've seen people make incredible strides in recovering their health, reconciling broken relationships, and achieving professional success that they had never known. I'm ready to help you do the same thing.

If you've read this far, you are likely a curious, ambitious, and sensitive person on the quest for a fuller and happier life. As I wrote this book, I had you in mind. As I said in the preface, it has taken me a lifetime of learning to be able to share this journey with you, and I know you will benefit greatly from the principles, practices, and methods that I've outlined in this book.

Albert Einstein once said that creativity is imagination having fun. So let's enjoy make big changes and have fun doing it.

CHAPTER 1

UNDERSTANDING YOUR MAGNIFICENT MIND

The energy of the mind is the essence of life.

—Aristotle

A re you facing overwhelming challenges? Do you feel like life is going nowhere but you would love to energize your emotions, potential, relationships, or achievement again? Does your life lack passion and purpose? Do you want to undergo a powerful renewal and get back on track to fulfilling your dreams? And what about your health? Are you in dis-ease? Would you like to be part of a growing company of people who are healed and feeling vibrant and healthful?

In 1955, *McCall's* magazine documented the story of Madame Bire, a woman who had been blind since birth. Predictably, her optic nerves were atrophied and incapable of working at all. During the visit to the healing waters in Lourdes, France, Madame Bire opened her eyes and could see for the first time. What made this even more astonishing is that when eye specialists later examined her, they discovered that her optic nerves were still atrophied, so by medical standards, she shouldn't have been able to see at all. Yet she had twenty-twenty vision with a pair of eyes that specialists considered dead. The power of Creative Intelligence within her worked a miracle that allowed her to see for the rest of her life.

Within you is this same power, capable of healing disease, giving perfect direction for your life, enabling you to manifest abundance, and providing you with a deep and lasting connection to the Divine. Creative Intelligence resides in the depth of your being and is already working day in and day out. It regulates your bodily functions, responds to your desires, and gives structure and purpose to every moment. Yet for you to access this inner storehouse of power, you must first understand what it is and how it works.

To build the world-famous Golden Gate Bridge in San Francisco, Joseph Strauss, a poet and engineer, had to learn everything he could about suspension bridges. He'd made his name building hundreds of drawbridges and a fifty-five-mile railroad bridge across the Bering Strait, but this was his first crack at a bridge of its design and dimension. While fighting the political battles necessary to get the permits to build the bridge, he threw himself into learning the latest about metallurgy and cable-suspension design. Working with experts to guide him along the way, he built the Golden Gate Bridge to international acclaim.

In many ways, the same is true for you as you launch into the exciting journey of creation, healing, and prosperity. You will need to learn the methods and technologies of miracles, but like Joseph Strauss, you aren't alone in this magnificent journey. Countless numbers of people have gone before you and manifested miracles[1] of healing, well-being, and

---

[1] One of my editors cautioned me against using the language of miracles throughout this work, suggesting that it was a "loaded word." After thought and conversation with my higher guides, I chose to keep it in because it communicates exactly what I want you to know. Whether miracles are merely a previously unknown natural process made manifest through the power of the mind or the intervention of transcendent powers from other realms, both

prosperity. They've left telltale tracks along the path, so you and I can confidently make this journey together.

Miracles Are Your Birthright

We live in exciting times as the mysteries of the universe are being revealed at a rate unknown before. Researchers are now studying and understanding transformations and healings—once relegated to the realm of miracles—as practical, transformative technologies are available to anyone who is willing to learn and apply their principles. While a trip to the healing shrine at Lourdes may be faith building and beneficial, we now know that the mind can release a host of healing chemicals and processes that will yield seemingly miraculous results in the comfort of one's living room. A pilgrimage to Delphi, the home of the ancient Oracle, who was believed to transmit messages from the gods, might stimulate a greater appreciation for transcendent wisdom, but you can develop your intuitive capacity to solve life's challenges in your own garden. And while you might enjoy a visit to the Shrine of the Seven Lucky Gods in Osaka, Japan, you can develop and sustain good fortune through the insight and prescient clarity of your own mind while seated at your desk or conference table.

I don't want to lose you here. I am not dismissing the power of religious faith. For years, I was an Episcopal priest and pastor, and I dedicated myself to helping people discover the power of a life lived in union with the Divine. As a matter of fact, I think that our religious and mythically inclined ancestors were on to something long before those of us with a materialistic bent. They knew, to paraphrase Shakespeare, that there are more things in heaven and on earth than are dreamed of in our philosophies. Countless thousands of people with active and compelling spiritual practices agree with Dr. Wayne Dyer, who taught that there is

---

are possible through the proper application of the principles that I will share in this book. So go ahead and expect miracles!

a spiritual answer to every problem. So, in many ways, people of faith believed in the power of transformation long before the rest of us.

Yet let's be honest. There are lots of people who seem to be miraculously healed but have little or no religious faith at all and many religious people who suffer all their lives with physical or emotional diseases and never seem to get relief. My point is this: spiritual practitioners across the ages discovered the power of interacting with the Creative Intelligence (which many call God) in a way that dramatically changed the course of their lives. And now, thanks to a greater understanding of how the body and mind interact, we can all find a way into this transformational process as well. That is the purpose of this book: to help you understand the power already active within you and to show you how to access the deep connection with Creative Intelligence that resides in your magnificent mind.

How Does Your Magnificent Mind Work?

Since we live in the century of the computer, it might be helpful to view your mind as an operating system that meets all your needs. From beating your heart and controlling your blood pressure to allowing you to write poetry or create intricate algorithms, your mind is hard at work supporting you. Later in this book, we'll examine the mind in a bit more depth to understand how it accomplishes these tasks, but for this introduction, let's just say that the operating system has two major functions or parts. We call these the *conscious* and the *subconscious* minds.

The conscious mind is the seat of our intellect, rational decision-making abilities, willpower, and logic. It is the day-to-day mind that makes our conscious decisions, does the laundry, and goes to parent-teacher conferences. The subconscious mind, on the other hand, is where our deep memories, emotions, impulses, passions, symbols, motivations, and mind-body connections pulsate with (for the most part) untapped power. When these two functions of the mind work in harmony, miracles occur, but unfortunately most people don't understand these two distinct yet necessary parts.

It's been estimated that the conscious mind contributes only about 10 percent to the power of the mind, while the subconscious brings 90 percent.[2] Part of the power of the subconscious is that it's where your life script is found. This life script, or subconscious programming, is a pattern of beliefs that was established in early childhood and has been refined over the course of your life by experiences and the meaning they provide. When you're running on autopilot without much conscious thought, it's in large part—for good and ill—thanks to the programmed patterns in your life script. The things that make us angry, the people that attract us, our taste in music, and our ability to handle frustration all flow from the programming of the subconscious mind.

The emerging science of neurophysiology, which is the study of the relationship between the mind and body, has revealed how economical the brain is when it comes to thought patterns. We know that each thought releases a chemical in the body, and if that thought is repeated often enough, an energetic and emotional default is established in the brain. This way, the brain doesn't have to waste a nanosecond processing old information and can be on the lookout for new data to interact with. These energy/emotional patterns drop into the subconscious and become part of the programming of your life. In other words, your past thinking becomes part of your present reality.

In large part, this accounts for why it is so difficult to make a change in habits or chart a new course for our lives and then stick to it. We decide—using our conscious mind—that we want to lose weight, stop smoking, regain sexual prowess, learn a language, master our finances, or find a new life partner. But when we come face-to-face with

---

[2] In his groundbreaking book *Professional Hypnotism Manual*, Dr. John Kappas suggests that the conscious mind is responsible for 12 percent of the mind's processing power and the subconscious for 88 percent. There are varying schools of thought in this regard, but for the sake of this work, I'm going to place the division of conscious/subconscious at 10/90 percent.

resistance to change, our willpower collapses, and we feel like we've had the rug pulled out from under us.

The reason for this is rather simple: we made the decision to change with the conscious mind, but we failed to make the necessary connections and changes in the subconscious, where our power of motivation resides. It's like the captain of an ocean liner standing at the helm of the vessel without understanding how the propulsion or navigation systems work. Without a functional knowledge of the ship, the captain is limited before the journey even begins. Reprogramming limiting subconscious patterns is the work of any therapist, hypnotist, or life coach. Without subconscious change, the clock starts ticking, and you revert to old, programmed patterns of thinking and feeling again and again.

In some ways, the process of change is simple. While we will explore it in greater depth later in this book, just know for now that to transform your life, you must first identify what you want to change and what beliefs keep the limiting patterns in place. Then, by accessing the subconscious mind, you disable the beliefs that have held you hostage and replace them with new and empowering beliefs. There are many methods to replace the old beliefs with the new and techniques to reinforce the changes that you make; but for now, suffice it to say that what you create is a whole new mind. That's why I call this the work of transformation; if we do our work correctly, a new person emerges on the other side of the process.

The Mind of Your Body

Another important thing to understand about the power of the mind to change your life is the connection between your mind and your body. Although Hippocrates suggested twenty-five centuries ago that there was a connection between a person's emotions and his or her physical health, the practice of medicine in the West today has largely been focused on what I call biology, bacteria, and betterment. In other words, the human body gets ill because of some infection or injury, and the way to treat it is by pharmaceutical medicine or surgery. Some cultures place far more value on the use of herbs and energy work in the healing process than we do, and history shows that there has always been a minority opinion within the medical community that there is a link between the inner and outer worlds of the patient. But at the turn of the twentieth century, respected medical voices began pointing out what now seems to be obvious: there is an absolute connection among mind, body, and spirit. For example, back in 1909, a physician named Richard Cabot, who worked with a primarily destitute population, wrote:

> I found myself constantly baffled and discouraged when it came to treatment. Treatment in more than half of the cases ... involved an understanding of the patient's economic situation and economic means, but still more of his mentality, his character, his previous mental and industrial history, all that brought him to his present condition in which sickness, fear, worry, and poverty were found inextricably mingled.

You are blessed to live in an era when the connection between your mind and body is becoming more accepted every day. The link between stress and somatic conditions like ulcers, insomnia, depression, and anxiety have been understood by physicians for some time, but now we know that stress can create or contribute to heart disease, asthma, obesity, diabetes, headaches, and Alzheimer's. We also have clinical proof that simple meditation techniques can reduce blood pressure, boost the immune system, decrease symptoms of premenstrual syndrome, increase fertility rates, and even double the amount of breast milk a mother can produce.

Dr. Joe Dispenza, in his work with patients who experience spontaneous remissions from debilitating and life-threatening disease, has shown how people can reverse these conditions through the power of their minds. While to most of us this is remarkable news, hypnotherapists have known for a long time that the way your body interacts with your environment is a function of your subconscious mind. To put it another way, we know that when your conscious mind thinks, it produces thoughts, but when the subconscious mind thinks, it produces feelings.

In her work on the "molecules of emotion," in 1997, Dr. Candace Pert, the chief of Brain Biochemistry at the National Institute of Health, made what (at the time) seemed to be an outrageous claim: our physical body is the expression of our subconscious mind. Science is confirming this position every day, and as we will learn in this book, our thoughts and feelings create the emotional/energy default that either keeps our bodies sick or propels them to phenomenal healing.

Psychoneuroimmunology studies the interaction between psychological processes and the nervous and immune systems of the body. While this highly scientific field produces lots of research studies that wouldn't make sense to you or me, Dr. Deepak Chopra has become a teacher for those of us trying to tap into this deep wisdom. He points out that emotions are the nexus point between mind and matter and that to heal our mind is to allow for the healing of our body as well. In the next chapter, on the placebo effect, I will share incredible stories with you about people who are healed through thought alone. Such is the power of your magnificent mind!

The Manifesting Mind

What do Napoleon Hill, James Allen, Joseph Murphy, Dale Carnegie, Louise Hay, Stuart Lichtman, Tom Paley, Catherine Ponder, Michael Beckwith, and Wayne Dyer have in common? They are accomplished in the field of personal and spiritual development and have proven that the human mind has the potential to manifest prosperity, well-being, and abundance. In these pages, we will demonstrate what they have discovered through a lifetime of study: that the mind is part of the alchemy of abundance. They also have shown us how to understand and perfect our application of timeless principles so we can have the results we desire.

I don't know about you, but for years I was under the impression that becoming a person of wealth and substance meant that I had to work my fingers to the bone. Well, as it turns out, that is simply not true. What's more true is that I must learn how to align my mind, heart, intent, and purpose to realize the success that is latent in my subconscious, only waiting for me to activate its power. This is not to say that to realize my dream, I won't have periods when I am taking massive, inspired action, but even that action is in response to my mind's guidance and direction for my own prosperity and well-being.

The Principles of Attraction

In so many ways, developing a manifesting mind is about learning the principles of attraction. Wayne Dyer, like many others, taught that abundance is not something we acquire; it is something we tune into. Let's use a faith-based analogy here: We live in God's abundant universe. There is no shortage of stars, oxygen, water, sunshine, grace, or love. So, for us to think boldly about how we might achieve and generously contribute to the healing of the world is not selfish but rather a reflection of Creative Intelligence, which who makes abundance possible. As we align with Creative Intelligence, not only do we find new paths of possibility open for us, we also draw to us those forces and people who help our dreams come true.

As with so many facets of our journey of empowerment, we most likely have subconscious blocks to the free flow of the energy of abundance. Perhaps we were taught in religious classes that it is more virtuous to be poor and dependent on God than to experience God's generosity. Or maybe our Depression-era parents told us at a very early age that "money doesn't grow on trees" and is therefore for other people, not us. Like any other impediment in our subconscious programming, these cognitive distortions can be overcome, and our mind can expand to see new possibilities for prosperity, which then allows us to live well and do good on a massive scale.

Summary

Are you as excited as I am about the journey of transformation that awaits us? In my workshops and seminars, I have the privilege of seeing people come to understand how their mind works and begin to apply it to make powerful change in their lives. We learn together, sometimes laughing and sometimes crying at the powerful revelations that come to us as we walk into well-being, liberation, and abundance. It is so much fun to see years drop off people's face when they realize they can enjoy their life every day and have prayers answered that they had long thought impossible.

In the next chapter, we are going to see how the placebo effect heals people without medicine or surgery. We will develop a more in-depth understanding of the ways that the mind works in its myriad and wonderful ways, and we will learn how to put body, mind, and spirit together to realign ourselves with the original purposes of the Creative Intelligence that we call God. We will discover how love and gratitude are the keys to unlock the deepest recesses of our hearts, and we will discover the power of our magnificent mind to heal the world. Join me, and let's get started now!

CHAPTER 2

PLACEBO POWER: YES, IT IS MIND OVER MATTER

*If the mind can heal the body, but the body can't heal the
mind, then the mind must be stronger than the body.*

—Dr. Helen Schuman, *A Course in Miracles*

The story of pseudonymous Mr. Wright has been told for years every
time the power of the mind to heal the body is discussed. It's worth
hearing the story again because it illustrates the exciting power of
your magnificent mind. Bruno Klopfer, a psychologist on the staff
of the UCLA Medical Center, mostly known for his work with the
Rorschach inkblot tests, published a paper about Mr. Wright, a patient
with advanced lymphoma. Wright was getting no medical relief from
any treatment and had developed large tumors in his neck, groin, and
armpits. His oncologist had given up hope that he would recover, but
Wright believed that there might be some breakthrough discovery to
help him.

Wright heard of an experimental drug called Krebiozen and
demanded that his doctor get some of the drug for him. Since his

case was so advanced, he didn't qualify to be part of the drug trials, but his persistence won the day, and he got his injection of Krebiozen on a Friday. By the next Monday, his condition was so improved that his tumors had been reduced to half their original size, and he was energized and happy. After ten days of this "miracle" cure, Wright was sent home to live a productive and happy life.

But then disaster struck. Two months after he'd been sent home, he read in the newspapers that Krebiozen was a medical and scientific failure. Within a matter of days, Wright relapsed, and the tumors returned. Desperate to save his patient's life, Wright's oncologist told him that the newspaper reports had been inaccurate and only the batch used in the study had been defective. This, the doctor said, was why the tumors had returned; it had been a weak dose of a bad batch. He went on to tell his patient that he had could procure a more highly refined and potent version of Krebiozen and asked Wright if he was willing to undergo the experimental treatment again.

Ever the optimist, Wright agreed to receive another dose of the medicine, so his doctor injected him with the "wonder drug." Unknown to Wright, however, his physician had injected him not with Krebiozen, but with saline solution. In short order, Wright's tumors vanished, and he was healthy and happy.

Two months later, the miracle drug Krebiozen was again in the news, this time being exposed not only as an ineffective medicine, but as nothing more than amino acids laced with mineral oil. The papers reported that the manufacturers of the drug were indicted and were slated for prosecution. Wright read this with dismay, and two days after returning to the hospital for further treatment, he died of lymphoma.

What are we to make of this story? Was it an overblown case of psychosomatic illness? Were his tumors and blood tests fake? Why was he able to think himself well then terminally ill then well, and then ill again? All the evidence available then was that Wright was in stage four, terminal lymphoma: the same disease that killed Jacqueline Kennedy Onassis, Ingrid Bergman, and Arlen Specter and eventually killed him as well. Yet, with the promise of a wonder drug, Wright was evidently able to transform all his physiology to bring about rapid and profound healing. Sadly, when the evidence for the drug crumbled, so did the platform of his faith, and he died from the disease from which he had recovered twice.

As you read these words, you may be experiencing a similar life-threatening illness and have looked far and wide for relief. Or maybe you're perfectly healthy, but you've been drawn to this book because you want to understand more about the power of your magnificent mind in other areas of your life. At this point in my workshops and seminars, I explain why we take the time to understand a little about the placebo effect.

Let's face it, we've been raised in an era of materialism and make decisions on evidence-based practices, so simple appeals to faith don't cut it for many. I tell my students that *if you become convinced that the mind is powerful enough to heal the body, you can also believe in its power in the other areas of your life as well.* The skeptic can write off another's professional success as the product of hard work or luck and reject the imaginative power of the mind. But put that same skeptic in the proximity of someone healed of an incurable disease like multiple sclerosis, and his or her faith in rationality is shaken to the core.

So, let's look at the mind's power to heal—what science calls the placebo effect. I guarantee that it will be a good read, and my hope is that it will help you have a greater appreciation for the height, depth, and breadth of the mind's power.

Just What Do We Know about the Placebo Effect?

Those who have studied the interaction between mind and body know that nonmedical healing has been around since the beginning of recorded history. Power centers and shrines have been places of healing for the faithful who seek to be made well. Faith healers are known in every religion as people who have a powerful connection to the Divine and so can cure the sick and bring peace of mind to the troubled. But miraculous powers weren't limited to religious healers. In the mid-1600s, King Charles II of England was said to have laid hands on over one hundred thousand people, many of whom were reported to be healed. The collective consciousness of that era held that kings and queens ruled by "divine right" and on occasion manifested "divine powers."

In the late 1700s, a physician named Franz Anton Mezmer discovered what he thought was a breakthrough in the healing power of the mind-body. He believed that the body contained a powerful fluid that he called "animal magnetism," which could be manipulated by placing and moving magnets over the patient's body to affect a cure. He took his research further and discovered that by looking deeply in patients' eyes and waving his hands around their body, he could induce a series of convulsions. When the patients woke awoke, they were healed of whatever malady brought them to Mezmer in the first place. He was convinced that it was the healer that had the power to make the change, and his technique came to be known as Mesmerism. But later research would prove that the change came from the transformed mind of the patient.

For the next one hundred years, physicians and hypnotists experimented with techniques to cure patients through the power of their mind alone. By evoking trance states in their subjects and offering powerful suggestions, many were inexplicably healed of diseases and physical defects.

Science Gets Involved

Fast-forward to World War II and the surgical tents of Dr. Henry Beecher who, when he ran out of painkillers, instructed his nurses to give patients injections of saline solution while telling them that they were receiving morphine. The patients who received the shots of water immediately relaxed and exhibited symptoms of being under the influence of the drug. Beecher was then able to perform emergency surgeries without complications.

Beecher wasn't the first medical doctor to use what later came to be called the placebo effect on a mass scale. James Esdaille, a Scottish surgeon who worked in India between 1843 and 1846, performed about four hundred major operations of all kinds, such as amputations, removal of tumors and cancerous growths, and operations on the eye, ear, and throat. All operations were conducted under what he called "mental anesthesia," and he reported that only 2 to 3 percent of his patients had any postoperative pain or infection.

When he left the army, Dr. Beecher authored a massive study to prove the power of suggestion when working with patients, and around 1955, civilian doctors began to offer sugar pills to patients who weren't responding well to conventional treatment. Some patients got better; some got worse. This purely biological method of pill-in-mouth without any explicit trance inductions was promising enough that more attention was given to research in the placebo effect as part of clinical drug trials.

A Breakthrough Moment

Of the hundreds of cases in medical literature about the placebo effect, I want to highlight three that illustrate the power of the mind to change our body chemistry. The first of these studies took place in 1978 when Dr. Jon Levine of the University of San Francisco changed forever how we think about mind-body medicine.

For this experiment, forty people who had just had their wisdom teeth removed were given injections of saline, although they were told they were getting painkillers. As you might imagine by now, most of the patients physically responded as if they had been given an opiate drug. After a while, the patients were given a second injection, this time of a drug called Naloxone, which blocks morphine and endorphins (natural painkillers) in the brain. The patients reported the onset of severe discomfort and were given the false painkillers again.

The fascinating thing this study revealed was that patients who thought they were getting painkillers by injection produced them through the power of their mind. If the saline shot had only relaxed the patients and helped psychologically manage their pain, then the Naloxone shouldn't have worked. But since the patients' brains produced opiates, there was something for the Naloxone to interact with. This was the first study to show that our minds can change our body chemistry and create what Dr. Norman Cousin's called "nature's perfect pharmacy" inside our own body.

The second example comes from Italy, where in 2003 Dr. Fabrizio Benedetti demonstrated the power of the mind over individual neurons in the brain. His study built on the work of a 2001 study in Canada, where Parkinson's patients were told that they were receiving medicine to help with their tremors, even though it was saline. Over half of them consistently had increased motor control and ability.

In his work, Benedetti injected the drug Sumatripitan to stimulate growth hormones in the brains of Parkinson's patients. He then conducted a brain scan on each of the patients and tracked how their brains lit up under the influence of the drug. He next administered a saline solution to the patients, telling them that it was sumatripitan.

Can you guess what the brain scans revealed? If you guessed their brains continued to light up in *the same* way as when they had been given the drug, you are correct. They had been conditioned to experience the effects of sumatripitan, so when they received the saline shot, their mind simply referred to the previous experience and continued to produce the hormones.

Example number three falls under the classification of what I'd call "weirder than weird." In 2010 a Harvard Medical School experiment gathered forty patients who suffered from irritable bowel syndrome (IBS) and asked them to participate in a "groundbreaking study." These patients were given a bottle marked "Placebo Pills" and told that while they were made of an "inert substance," they produced positive effects with IBS patients. A second group was given no pills at all.

At the end of three weeks, those patients who took the placebo pills showed twice as much relief from their IBS symptoms than those who took nothing. In other words, they knew the pills were placebos, but because they had been told that they worked, the patient's bodies experienced radical change.

Do You Need Prozac?

In 1998, Dr. Irving Kirsch of the University of Connecticut conducted what researchers called a meta-analysis of the effectiveness of antidepressant drugs. He was shocked to discover that in nineteen drug trials, most of the improvement to the 2,300 participants was due not to antidepressants but to the placebo effect of suggestion and inert pills.

Using the power of the Freedom of Information Act, he discovered that the pharmaceutical industry had unpublished reports that showed that placebos worked as well as Prozac, Effexor, Serzone, and Paxil 81 percent of the time. He discovered that the only time prescription drugs did better was with severely depressed people; otherwise, the evidence showed that you can get well as much from thinking "correctly" as you can by taking a pill.

As you might imagine, the pharmaceutical industry immediately challenged his work, but ultimately his methodology was proven sound, and the facts stand today as he discovered a decade ago.

So, What Do You Think?

So far, we've performed what pilots who practice landings call a touch-and-go, using three examples of the mind positively changing the body. In the first case, we saw how the brain produced its own painkillers, in the second how it released hormones to bring relief, and in the third how suggestion alone brought about an alleviation of IBS symptoms. In his book *You Are the Placebo*, Dr. Joe Dispenza goes into cases like these and more with the precision of a medical researcher, and yet he makes the material accessible to the average reader. He has done us a high service and is transforming how we think of mind-body interaction. I highly recommend the book.

But this is just the beginning when it comes to mind-body healing. In two non-pharmaceutical cases, surgeons led their patients to believe that they were going to conduct surgery, when in two instances they did little—yet all the patients got better. In the first case, a surgeon operated on three groups of patients who had severe osteoarthritis of the knee. With the first two groups, he performed one of two reparative surgeries on them, while on the third group he merely made the surgical incisions and then sewed them back up. If you've hung in with me this far, I'm sure you're able to guess what happens next: all three groups reported successful recovery and were walking fine years later.

In 1959, surgeons performed open-heart surgery on two groups of patients who were suffering from angina (chest pain). The first group received the internal mammary ligation procedure designed to increase blood flow, while those in the second group (as was the case with the knee patients) were opened and closed without the procedure and sent to the recovery room. The results of these surgeries stunned the researchers. Sixty-seven percent of the patients who had the usual surgery got significantly better, but 83 percent of the sham surgery patients were profoundly improved.

What is the one constant throughout all these examples of recovery and renewal? It wasn't the type of cases or the methods of the experiments used. As we saw in the last two examples, recovery didn't come from taking an inert pill or having a phony injection. The one common denominator in all of the examples we've looked at was the belief of the patient. Each of them believed that the "treatment" would work, and for most of them it did. Belief—that is, an opinion held with certitude—allowed the mind to respond in ways that produced sometimes miraculous healing.

Beware the Nocebo Effect

The Latin word *placebo* can be translated as "I will please," while the word *nocebo* is translated as "I will harm." History is filled with examples of people experiencing horrible effects to their health and sanity by believing the negative suggestions of authority figures. The nocebo effect is a way to understand the power of curses and black magic upon people. Anthropologists tell us of the deadly results of the curses of witch doctors or voodoo practitioners; when hapless people believed the words of the authority figure, they often experienced exactly what had been "cast" at them.

But you don't need to go to the swamps of the bayou or to tribal cultures to see the power of the nocebo effect. In a Japanese study in 1962, children who were identified as being highly allergic to poison ivy had one arm rubbed with poison ivy but were told that it was a harmless leaf. Ninety percent of those children experienced no allergic response to the poison ivy. But when their other arm was rubbed with a harmless leaf, and they were told it was poison ivy, all had allergic reactions.

In another experiment, forty asthma patients were given inhalers containing nothing but clear vapor, but they were told that it contained an allergy-inducing substance. Many of them experienced allergic responses in their respiratory systems, and a third went into full-blown asthma attacks. Those conducting the experiments rushed to give the people in respiratory distress a new inhaler (full of water vapor only) and told them that this would relieve their symptoms quickly. Universally this new inhaler opened the passageways of the test subjects, and they were well again.

The nocebo effect is what inspired me to study the power of mind-body interactions. I have friends and family members who have been told by their doctors that they would never walk, make music, have an erection, or some other function again. Given our cultural dependence on the authority of physicians, I have seen people given death sentences in the medical office and then, like Mr. Wright in the beginning of the chapter, go home and die. But with the advent of alternative medicines, hypnotic inductions, and the testimony of people who have overcome the deadly prophecy of doctors, a new consciousness is emerging that challenges the existing way of thinking about health, illness, and death.

In the next chapter, I will tell a story about how, by understanding the power of the mind and the way it works, people have reversed the aging process and experienced a new vibrancy and vitality to life. And we will touch on one of the reasons we can make such powerful changes in our bodies—that is, by understanding just a little about the emerging science of epigenetics.

I hope this quick overview has given you a new perspective on the power of your mind and is stimulating you to think new thoughts about yourself. It sure seems that, when it comes to change, nothing is off the table anymore.

Summary

The ability of people to heal themselves by nonmedical practices has long been known by people of faith and those willing to step outside of conventional medical traditions. Overwhelming evidence is beginning to emerge to show that through the proper alignment of mind and body, people can heal themselves.

We've seen case studies where people have taken inert pills and saline injections and have been healed as if they had taken medicine. We've seen sham surgeries resulting in recoveries as good or better than those people who had real surgical procedures, and we've seen how the power of the mind is as effective in treating some types of mental disorders as medications have ever been. We've also discovered the power of the nocebo effect—that is, the power of negative pronouncements or fake medical procedures that produced harm to those subjected to them. The mind is powerful, and subsequent generations of people will benefit from mental therapies alone.

CHAPTER 3

UNLOCKING THE SECRETS OF YOUR MAGNIFICENT MIND

The thing always happens that you really believe in; and the belief in a thing makes it happen.

—*Frank Lloyd Wright*

In many ways, I believe that we are living in what historian's call an axial age—that is, the discoveries of the power of the mind made in the last decades will transform how we live in the years to come. While a full understanding of spontaneous remissions of debilitating diseases and the placebo effect is still in its infancy, we are seeing *proof* that the mind is more powerful than we ever thought. We are now hearing stories of prosperity and manifestation that seemed impossible, and we feel deep in our hearts that we stand at the cutting edge of a radically new way of living.

As with all breakthrough periods, our great-grandchildren will take for granted the things we are discovering today. It's not only possible but likely they will know that to make powerful change, the first place to go is deep within their own minds to activate their imagination. They will *know* that all prosperity, health, and success is created first within and then realized in the outer world. Future generations will know that removing energetic blocks and connecting peace of mind, imagination, and strong positive emotions regularly will bring about change that our parents worked so hard to realize.

Education in the future might revolve around learning not only how to work with the conscious mind but also how to tap the subconscious and collective mind to interact with a greater wisdom than their own. What is revolutionary for us will be history to them, and they will benefit from the brave work that we are doing now.

In the previous chapters, I hope I've stimulated your interest in understanding more about the power of your magnificent mind. So far, we've looked at the incredible potential to transform your life so you experience new joy, hope, purpose, and passion. In my own work, I have seen people completely change their direction, and I believe you can have this experience as well.

All you need to do is browse the self-improvement aisles of your local bookstore or spend about thirty seconds on Amazon.com to see the hunger of people who are searching for more. We are no longer content with an average life; we want to expand our consciousness and to experience deep fulfillment, joy, and success.

So now comes the fun part. Rather than just learning about what a "new mind" means for others, let's put this knowledge to work transforming *your* relationships, career, spirituality, and personal bottom line. Without a doubt, I can promise you that if you learn how to access the powerhouse of your mind and commit to applying the principles you learn here, you will be a different person in a year.

How can I make such a bold claim? Because besides seeing transformation happen in others, I've lived through the process of re-creation and renewal in my own life. Ten years ago, I was bankrupt and addicted to drugs and alcohol (yes, while an Episcopal priest). My personal and professional relationships were in ruins. Now I have a thriving transformational practice in Beverly Hills, am free of substance addictions, have fulfilling family connections, and am traveling the world speaking to thousands about the miracle of the magnificent mind. You are no different from me. Follow the path laid out in these pages, and you will transform your life as well.

How the Magnificent Mind Works

In the Paris of the late nineteenth century, Pierre Janet, a man considered to be one of the founding fathers of psychology, coined the term *subconscient,* which was later translated into English as *subconscious.* He said that as he worked with people, he discovered an entire level of awareness that lay beneath the day-to-day of conscious activity. From that jumping-off point, psychologists began to explore what one called the "netherworld" of the human mind. Researchers understood early on that the human mind was more multifaceted and complex than the "what do you want to have for lunch" processes of daily life. Studying patients in depth, Sigmund Freud and Carl Jung developed theories of the subconscious that are held by many psychiatrists and psychologists to this day.

You don't have to be a clinician to appreciate that something is going on, consciousness-wise, in your life. The fact that you are reading this tells me that you are thoughtful and engaged in a quest for a greater life than can be had by subsisting on *People* magazine, and it's this passion that excites me.

The Operating System of Your Mind

Over the course of the years, psychologists and psychiatrists have developed a basic theory of mind. For the sake of keeping it simple—and you engaged—let's look at the highlights together. To begin with, it's important to understand that while we have only one mind, it has two processes, or levels of operation: the conscious and the subconscious.

(Explorers in the field of consciousness and its impact on the body have identified the mind-body and have even discovered that the heart exhibits its own intelligence. We'll consider some of this later.)

The conscious, or objective, mind provides us with the ability to function daily. The conscious mind is the seat of logic, decision making, willpower, analytical ability, and judgment. If you want to decide which movie to see, you use the conscious mind. Likewise, if you want to drive your car, write a report, read blueprints, or argue a case in court, you use the conscious mind. The conscious mind operates through logical analysis, verbal language, facts, figures, and superficial memory. You are probably the most familiar with the conscious mind because, in many ways, as a twenty-first-century Western person, it's the only way of thinking in which you've been trained.

In his book *The Biology of Belief,* Dr. Bruce Lipton points out that one of the limitations of the conscious mind is that it processes information only at forty bits a second. In the supercomputing world of the mind, that's slower than the old dialup Internet connections. As we'll see, the conscious mind is significantly less powerful than the subconscious mind.

As with most areas of research, opinions vary, but there is a fundamental agreement that the conscious mind works with only 5 to 12 percent of the mind's total capacity. This explains, in large part, why powerful and lasting change is so difficult. It's like trying to play a piano masterpiece with one or two fingers; you can certainly knock out the basic melody, but that's as far as you'll get. In a moment, we'll see why most people can't overcome fear, lose weight, or craft a new life based on decisions and willpower alone. To power massive change, you can't rely on the AA battery of the conscious mind.

I'm not dismissing the importance of the conscious mind; without it we couldn't exist in the day-to-day world. It is through the conscious mind that we build cities, write computer code, work in the stock market, interpret x-rays and develop budgets. The men of Apollo 11 flew to the moon, landed there, and flew home thanks to the abilities of the conscious minds of thousands of people. I write this book and you are reading it thanks to our conscious minds. On the other hand, the motivations for me to write and you to read these pages springs from a far deeper source, and it's to that power center we now turn.

Introducing the Subconscious Mind

A forty-three-year-old client came to see me because she wanted to stop smoking, and she'd heard that hypnosis was a good way to do it. As she shared her story, she told me that neither of her parent smoked. She related that she began to smoke when she was eleven years old, chiefly due to the pressure of her older sister, who wanted an ally in rebellion. Her sister introduced her to all the "cool kids" at school, who would sneak off to smoke every chance they could. At first, she liked neither the taste nor smell of cigarettes, but she was thrilled with the positive attention she got from girls that she looked up to. So in no time she was hooked, and she embarked on her thirty-two-year career as a smoker.

Like many people who have tried repeatedly to stop smoking, my client had limited success in breaking free of tobacco's stranglehold. She studied all the negative effects that smoking had on her life: shortened life expectancy, heart disease, high blood pressure. She read that there are over four thousand chemicals compounds in a single cigarette, and she knew that nothing but trouble awaited her with every puff of smoke.

So, time after time, she made a promise that after the next cigarette she would quit, praying for help. She tried low-nicotine cigarettes, vaping, gums, patches, affirmations, and exercise but never had consistent success. She came to me frustrated and angry at herself for being so "weak willed," and she couldn't understand why she couldn't stop. In other words, she had used all the resources of her conscious mind and repeatedly met with disappointment and failure.

I explained to her how her addiction to cigarettes had little to do with her physical addiction to tobacco. We know that physical dependence on nicotine diminishes over time and is usually gone by the third day after you have smoked your last cigarette. For most people, the struggle with tobacco is rooted in habit, emotion, conditioning, and belief—in other words, in the subconscious mind.

In my client's case, her subconscious received a lifetime of suggestions from the conscious mind, such as cigarettes make me cool; I find comfort when I'm smoking; and I have the support of people who care about me. The list could go on, but ultimately her subconscious mind was so committed to her role as a smoker that it was determined that she continue down the path of addiction.

The subconscious is the part of our mind where our feelings, emotions, intuitions, and personal power reside. If the conscious mind uses language to communicate, the subconscious mind uses symbols and feelings. Anything that emerges from the depths of us, whether it is music or poetry, passion or motivation, comes from the subconscious mind. Her deep feeling of being hooked on cigarettes was rooted in a story that her subconscious guarded like a hidden fortune.

When we were looking at the conscious mind, we saw that it consisted of 5 to 12 percent of the mind's processing capacity. This means that the subconscious is the powerhouse controlling anywhere from 88 to 95 percent of our personal power and interactions with our world.

Again, thanks to Dr. Lipton, we know that the subconscious processes forty million bits of data per second. This accounts for its power, especially when compared to the forty bits of data per second of the conscious mind. It is a startling realization to discover that for all your thinking that you are in charge of your life, the truth is that your emotional response to just about everything is based on your subconscious programming.

Dr. James Murphy, a Divine Science minister based in Los Angeles, studied and taught about the power of the subconscious mind for thirty years. He got his professional start as a Jesuit priest, but when he healed himself of cancer using the power of his subconscious mind, he had to find a new spiritual context from which to grow. When few people understood the power of the subconscious mind, Dr. Murphy seemed to have preternatural insight into its workings. In 1963 he wrote:

> The infinite intelligence within your subconscious mind can reveal everything you need to know at every moment of time and point of space provided you are open-minded and receptive. You can receive new thoughts enabling to you bring forth new inventions, make new discoveries, write new books or plays. ... Through the power of your subconscious mind you can attract the ideal companion, as well as the right buyer for your home, and provide you with all the money you need, and the financial freedom to be, do and go as your heart desires. (*The Power of Your Subconscious Mind*)

Fifty years ago, Murphy understood things about the subconscious mind that science is just now discovering. Duke University and the Stanford Research Institute conducted studies of the subconscious mind and its ability to detect the thoughts of other people from a distance, the power of clairaudience, and extrasensory perception. In one of Dr. Joe Dispenza's conferences, he discovered a woman sitting in a large auditorium, facing front toward the platform, with her eyes closed, "watching" the staff in the back of the room and reporting their activities accurately. Things that seemed possible only to mystics and miracles workers in the past are now being attributed to the interaction between the conscious and the subconscious minds.

Let's go back to my client who had tried repeatedly but unsuccessfully to quit smoking. I explained to her that her subconscious was formed in earnest from the time of infancy till about nine years of age. Every time she had an experience, her mind created an association for it. For example, if as child her parents rewarded her with chocolate cake when she had done something well, her subconscious mind would have come to believe chocolate cake is good.

Obviously, the driver was not so much the chocolate cake as it was the good feelings the parental affirmation created—but the cake became the symbol of the approval. If this experience was repeated enough, her subconscious mind created what neurobiologist call an associative memory, and a psychological pattern of comfort was formed.

While this process of experience and association happens rapidly in childhood, it continues all our lives. When a strong experience or emotion breaks through the mind's defense system (more on this later), it becomes implanted in the subconscious. The more it is reinforced by repetitive thought and behavior, the stronger it gets.

This explains why people who suffer from eating disorders struggle with their relationship to food; their subconscious mind believes in the safety and reward patterns that eating activates. The person who is addicted to food experiences stress, which activates his or her sympathetic nervous system (we lay folks call it the fight-flight-or-freeze syndrome), and his or her subconscious mind looks for the associative memory to relieve the stress.

In this case, the associative memory that promises relief from this stress is food, so the person eats, and this activates the parasympathetic nervous system, which brings relief and comfort—for the moment. Sunny Sea Gold, in her book *Food: The Good Girl's Drug: How to Stop Using Food to Control Your Feelings,* gives a heartfelt and easily accessible story that illustrates this theory.

The same mechanism of stress-trigger-object-relief is just as real for people with any substance or process addiction. At some point, a powerful association was made in the subconscious mind that alcohol, marijuana, sex, shopping, shoplifting, religion, or adrenaline would reduce stress, conflict, anxiety, or fear. And the more that person engages the addictive process, the stronger the association in the subconscious that it is a "good thing."

We know that the power of the subconscious mind is vast and pervasive. On the one hand, it ensures that the primary bodily functions, like breathing, circulation, and temperature, function without conscious attention. But it also reinforces and sustains experiences within that become conditioned patterns. One person may have the "chocolate cake good" association while another might be repulsed by it. Both are due to conditioned patterns within the subconscious mind.

Part of the subconscious mind's role is to protect us from harm, so in addition to creating positive associations, it creates negative ones. If, as children, we were bit by a dog, hit by a car, or awakened in the night while being dragged from a burning house, the subconscious creates a strong association around the event that will be triggered for the rest of our lives unless they are changed.

As a child, I was on a road trip with my family, and we stopped at a famous split-pea soup restaurant on the coastal highway in California. Everybody was having a great time but me because somewhere between Los Angeles and Santa Barbara, I'd come down with a case of the flu. My fever was raging, and my stomach was very upset as we sat down for lunch. My father demanded that I eat the split-pea soup and enjoy it—dammit. About halfway through the meal, I became so sick, I just made it to the restroom in time to vomit it all up.

Afterward, feeling cleaned up but awful, I returned to the table, and my dad demanded that I finish the soup. I begged to have just a piece of bread, but he threatened to take me outside and spank me "within an inch of my life" if I didn't eat the soup. I ate the soup, got sick in the restroom again, and we went along on the rest of our vacation.

Can you guess what my visceral response to split-pea soup is today? Such is the power of negative associations in the subconscious mind.

People who come to my office because they can't find a life partner often discover that they have negative associations about being in intimate relationships. As we delve into their history, we discover powerful negative associations about relationships, and we learn how the subconscious "protects" them from intimacy. Erectile dysfunction or premature ejaculation in men and vaginisimus in women are physical examples of the way that the subconscious mind uses the body to block intimacy.

But there are subtler programmed responses that keep people from finding the love they desire. So back to my client who wanted to stop smoking. Her initial negative physical reaction to inhaling poison was overcome with stronger subconscious associations of comfort, acceptance, and belonging to people who cared for her. After a short while, nicotine released enough feel-good chemicals in her nervous system that a physical and emotional signature formed in her brain that hooked her on cigarettes.

The work before us was to expose beliefs that didn't serve her anymore and access the subconscious mind to change her associations about smoking. We had to introduce new and powerful suggestions that there was nothing to fear about giving up the old patterns around smoking, and then she had to learn new ways to relate to stress and activate the parasympathetic nervous system. Now, months later, she is an air-breather (ex-smoker) and is engaged in the process of enjoying her life.

The Creative Power of the Subconscious Mind

I hope it's clear by now that I have a deep and abiding respect for the power of the subconscious mind to solve many of the problems we face in our personal life. As a matter of fact, if I had a motto to print on a business card, it would be "Anything your mind creates it can recreate." I believe that there isn't a problem that can't be helped, overcome, or realigned by using the subconscious mind as it was created to be used.

Being an optimist, I also want to take just a minute here to encourage you to develop a positive relationship to your subconscious mind and allow it to be a powerful resource for good in your life. There's a saying in the hypnotic community: "The conscious mind thinks with words, while the subconscious mind thinks with feelings." Imagine the power of having your subconscious as your ally in the creative processes of your life. It's from the depths of one's subconscious mind that symphonies emerge, great poetry is written, beautiful art is created, and vibrant and passionate love is found. So it's fair to say that Michelangelo, Bach, Monet, and all the artists you know and love were deeply in touch with their subconscious mind, even if they didn't have a twenty-first-century psychology to articulate it.

Your subconscious is your connecting point to universal wisdom that some call God, and as such, messages come to you through dreams, visions, déjà vu moments, and images that arise while listening to beautiful music or when eating a delicious meal. In other words, your 90 percent mind is waiting to pluck you from your black-and-white world and deliver you into a magical world of beauty, color, creativity, vision, and love.

The Superconscious Mind and "The Field"

Above I have offered you a pretty accepted vision of the conscious and subconscious minds. Whether we adapt metaphors like conductor (conscious mind) and orchestra (subconscious mind) or ship captain (conscious mind) and propulsion system (subconscious mind), the field of hypnotherapy sees the mind as a process. One author states explicitly that the mind is the "brain at work," and yet the insights of quantum physics and alternative medicine are beginning to blur the boundaries that many of us thought were present in dealing with the mind.

For many medical practitioners, especially visionaries like Deepak Chopra and Andrew Weil, talking about the mind as being separate from the body is as out of date as bleeding patients with leaches to cure disease. The emerging language of such medicine refers to the mind-body and views the actions of the mind as influencing the body in ways that we didn't think were possible.

As I suggested before, we know that each thought releases a cascade of hormones and interacts with all our physical systems for good or ill. This explains, in large part, why the placebo effect works so powerfully;

mind affects matter. So, to see the body-mind as an integrated whole is a more accurate and effective way to practice medicine in the twenty-first century.

Quantum physics has revealed that at its most elementary levels, all of creation, ourselves included, is energy. Going even further, some experts in this field suggest that all of creation as we know it is joined together as a holistic web of energy. In this view, while maintaining a semblance of solidity and individuality, we are part of the collective energy systems of the universe. Author John Kehoe speculates that when we use our minds to become proficient with the universal energy web, we can access the energy and wisdom of Jesus, Buddha, Kwan-Yin, Albert Einstein, and any other being because we are all in the same web together.

Thus the emergence of transpersonal hypnotherapy suggests that our minds are a field, not only within our body, but within the whole of creation as well. And as we develop the ability to access and use this universal energy, we will be able to work wonders in our lives and in our worlds. All of this is currently at the level of theory and experiment, but it does explain why some beings could change water into wine, see into the past and future, raise the dead, and heal disease with a single touch. It will be fascinating to see how these thoughts are developed over the coming years.

What Do You Think?

Although we have just begun to understand how your magnificent mind works, you now have some idea of the opportunities for transformation that await you. We've seen that while you have only one mind, it has two distinct and different functions. Your conscious mind gives you the powers of logic, analysis, decision making, and willpower. It allows you to plan, prepare, and execute your life. But we've also seen that 95 percent of the time, the real driver of your experience is your subconscious mind. We've discovered that the subconscious records each experience that we have and then integrates that experience and the association as part of our programmed conditioning.

Your subconscious is the storehouse of emotions, intuition, motivation, and your contact with the Divine. The wisdom so necessary to thrive comes from the subconscious, and from its depths you can receive life-changing insights or career-elevating ideas. Using the power of your subconscious, you can visualize success in your mind and bring it to pass in your life. By accessing the power of your subconscious and changing patterns of belief, you can create luck and vibrant health. You can bring love into your life, and you can serve your family, friends, and the world at an explosive level.

Your subconscious mind is a faithful servant who awaits your commands to put it into action. So far, your input into the subconscious has probably been less than intentional, but now I am going to show you how to direct the orchestra of your mind to achieve magnificent results. In the next chapter, we will discover the things that block our creative power and find a way to release their magnetic pull. We will learn how your body is designed to work with your mind to bring success, and we will get a taste of that interaction. So, let's take a deep breath, turn the page, and jump!

Summary

This chapter has offered an introductory look at the way your mind functions. We've seen that the mind has two separate functions: the conscious and subconscious. The conscious mind is the realm of our logical, analytical, and directive self, while the subconscious is the home of our emotions, habits, life scripts, and motivations. While the conscious mind functions in a linear and verbal manner, the subconscious mind is formed by experiences and associations to those experiences. We asked the question "Why is the subconscious mind so powerful?" and we discovered that it is responsible for over 90 percent of our mind's power.

We've seen that thoughts are the result of the conscious mind thinking, while feelings are evidence that we are engaged with the subconscious mind. Through the proper use of both aspects of our magnificent mind, we can make the powerful and lasting changes we desire.

CHAPTER 4

PUTTING YOUR MAGNIFICENT MIND TO WORK FOR YOU

Whatever you determine to be true in the subconscious becomes true for you.

—Richard Hatch

The human mind is one of the most complex and wonderful systems of which we are aware. While not part of our anatomy (like the brain), the mind is energy in motion, and it makes us unique and precious. The mind creates symphonies, rockets, and corporations. It creates war and launches peace accords. It enables relationships and destroys them. Everything in existence was first in the mind of its creator. Bill Gates and Steve Jobs had competing ideas for personal computing, and both ideas hold sway over the technology world today. Jesus had an idea that he called "the kingdom of God," and Karl Marx had an idea that he entitled *The Communist Manifesto*. Religions and politics have long known the power of the mind and have sometimes used it for good and other times for ill.

As I alluded to earlier, our times are unique in that we have a greater understanding of the function and purpose of the mind than ever before, and we can program our minds to create the wonders of the world. So, in this chapter you are going to learn how to fully use both aspects of the mind to bring the change you want. In this book, I'm introducing you to accessing your deep inner power by using your conscious and subconscious minds to access your deep inner power.

Understanding the Subconscious in Six Easy Steps

As I pointed out in the last chapter, your mind has one purpose and two functions, or processes. While the conscious mind is the *you* of your "day-to-day" identity, the subconscious mind ensures that what *you* want, *you* get. Here are six things to know about the working of your subconscious mind and application points to make the information relevant to your growth and transformation.

1. Your subconscious is always on duty.

Since the subconscious is the part of your mind responsible for basic bodily functions, like breath and circulation, it's always on duty. Even after you are exhausted from a long day at work or play and drop into bed, the subconscious mind continues its protective and regulative functions. While you sleep, the subconscious is hard at work processing the information and experience from the previous day and getting you ready to excel in the day to come.

Please remember: In those moments when you feel like you are lost or struggling to find the answer to a crucial problem in your life, take a deep relaxing breath and know that your deepest mind is on the job. In no time, you'll have your answer if you follow the techniques outlined in this book.

2. Your subconscious mind records everything—always.

In an article by Amy Morin in *Psychology Today* magazine, it was estimated that the average person has about seventy thousand thoughts a day. From the insignificant "yogurt or eggs for breakfast?" to the profound "oh, here's the cure for cancer," our brain processes information all day long, and the subconscious mind reviews, filters, and stores everything that supports our preprogrammed patterns.

Have you ever been suddenly aware of and emotional discomfort and can't understand where it's coming from? The likely answer is that the subconscious mind encountered a thought or experience that conflicted with your programmed feeling patterns, and hence the strange feeling. It is as though the subconscious saw danger and released feelings of discomfort as a warning.

> *Please remember: Your subconscious mind holds everything you've ever stored there, ready to be used in support of your programming. Whether you've lost your keys or need to remember intricate law cases for the bar exam, if you've experienced, known, or felt something, it's there and can be recalled when you need it.*

3. The language of your subconscious mind is primarily symbolic.

When you are thinking about what to order on the breakfast menu or are engaged in a political discussion with your friends at dinner, you are using the verbal language feature of your conscious mind. For most of us, language is free-flowing and easy; we can form thoughts and express them to others. This isn't the case for some people who've had strokes. They can formulate thoughts, but the part of the brain that is used to express those thoughts has been damaged, so they struggle to speak a single word. When studying the subconscious mind's primary language, it's important to remember that its language is symbolic, metaphorical, and emotional. While we use verbal language to communicate to the subconscious mind, very often its response to us is in images and feelings.

That's why our dreams are symbolic and at times nonsensical; the subconscious expresses itself through feelings and symbols. If you take a dream analysis workshop, you learn how to interpret symbols and the messages behind them. Rarely can you take a dream at face value because it's using a different language than the language you use in your waking world. In dreams, neither a rooster nor your long-lost cousin have anything to do with roosters or cousins, but about drives, impulses, aspirations, and fears. So, to get the most from your dreamtime, you need to learn your personal symbolic dictionary. In like manner, world-class artists, poets, and musician's access their subconscious minds in a way that most of us can't (but could if we knew how) to move, inspire, and amaze us.

In my work with men who suffer from erectile dysfunction, we see that the inability to perform physically is often a symbolic representation of a disempowering belief lodged in the subconscious. If there is no physical reason why someone can't have an erection (like nerve damage or reduced blood flow due to hypertension medications), we look at where else in life the man struggles with potency. Often, a man feels his personal power is under assault at work or with his love partner.

When we understand the block and introduce simple visualizations and hypnotic reprogramming, the client is "standing at attention" in no time. In his book *Metaphors of Healing, Playful Language in Psychotherapy and Everyday Life,* Harish Malhotra shares hundreds of healing metaphors that he has created for use with his patients in therapy and that have yielded positive results. It is a good read, and I highly recommend it.

Please remember: Verbal language may allow you to write a story, but the images, symbols, and feelings that emerge from the subconscious mind allow the story to win the award. As we learn the power of symbol and metaphor and allow them to guide us, we equip ourselves to rise above our peers in every endeavor.

4. Your subconscious mind takes everything literally.

A story found in the March 8, 1952, edition of the *Canberra Times* newspaper highlights the power of the subconscious mind and makes a point worth remembering. The newspaper told the story of a British man who had a young daughter that suffered from debilitating arthritis and psoriasis of the skin. This concerned father repeatedly told anyone who would listen, "I would give my right arm to have my daughter healed."

One day, while driving his car, the father and daughter were in a terrible car crash. While both survived, the father's right arm was amputated at the shoulder. After both father and daughter were stabilized at the local hospital, the daughter discovered that her arthritis and psoriasis were gone. This incredible story, researched by a British medical society before publication, leads me to ask, did the father's subconscious mind facilitate the accident so that his desire to trade his arm for his daughters could be realized? Or had the daughter heard her father's desire spoken enough that when his arm was severed, her subconscious mind healed her? We'll never know, but this is only one of many examples of how the subconscious mind takes you literally.

When clients come into the hypnotherapy office for pain management, we often discover that their pain is a symbolic representation of an unhealed emotional pattern in their lives. When there is no physical reason for pain, we have discovered that these "body syndromes" are often the subconscious mind's way of calling out for emotional healing and integration.

Just think of the language that we use to describe the troublesome person who is a "pain in the neck" or an upsetting relationship that "gives me heartburn." Sometimes, by simply putting the client into a hypnotic state, we discover what is trying to be healed, and when addressed, the pain disappears.

So, students of transformation learns quickly to watch what they say as the subconscious mind, ever the faithful servant, seeks to create the reality that it hears in the words that we say.

> *Please remember: Becoming conscious of what we say and how we say it is both revelatory and transformative. When we truly understand the power of our words, we partner with our subconscious minds to create the reality we desire.*

5. Your subconscious mind knows only the present time.

Earlier in this book, when we looked at the functions of the conscious mind, we discovered that among its many gifts to us is the ability to think logically and analytically. In the much-used metaphor of the bicameral brain, we are told that people who are right-brained are emotional, creative, and more in touch with feelings than their left-brained counterparts, who are logical, rational, analytical, and more connected to their thoughts. While there is emerging evidence in neuroscience to suggest that both sides of our brains have the capacity to do it all, it is true that we can be logical and rational as the result of our conscious mind.

Because of this, it's safe to say that the subconscious mind does not think in the space-time continuum of the conscious mind. That's why, although you may be forty-five years old, when you have dreams of yourself as a little child or as a senior citizen, it feels real upon awakening. That's also why, when an old pattern or life script is activated within, you might feel like a child again, vulnerable, afraid, or needy. The subconscious mind knows only now, so when it encounters strong memories of the past or fantasies of the future, it reacts in ways that seem irrational and, to the conscious mind, a little absurd.

This now-ness of the subconscious mind is part of its genius and is a process that we put to good use in transformational work. In the next chapter, we are going to begin not only crafting a vision for your life, but also "downloading" it using strong positive emotion. Do this enough, and the subconscious pattern changes and a new way of being in the now occurs as you begin to think with a new mind.

Popular speaker and teacher Eckhart Tolle reminds us that "the present moment is the power moment." This is in large part because when we access the power of the subconscious mind and join it to the possibilities of the infinite, we can work wonders. Because there is no past or future to the subconscious mind, the now becomes our playground of creation.

> *Please remember: By becoming comfortable with the subconscious mind's one-pointed attention on the present moment, we can enter past and future and create a transformational paradigm that we can use again and again to bring about powerful change.*

6. Your subconscious mind creates your reality out of its program.

If this point isn't crystal clear by now, let's just take a moment to call attention to it again. From the day of our birth, our subconscious mind has been collecting and cataloging all the experiences of our life and creating programs that enable us to interact with and make sense of the outer world. If the consistent message that our subconscious received was "food makes emotional pain go away," it creates patterns of impulse and response that drive us to eat when we are stressed out. If we were abused in childhood by men who were supposed to care for us, our reality becomes "Men cause pain. Avoid them at all costs!"

In this way, the subconscious is not creative at all. Like a well-operating computer, it acts on its hardware and software to produce the programs of patterned response that we are so used to. But having said this, it's important to know that this vast potential to create reality can be channeled for our good to make, as the Bible puts it, "all things new."

While the subconscious is the point of our programming, exciting new research is showing that it is the access point to a larger sense of mind than we've been used to before. Spiritual people would call this our openness to the Divine, and as we saw in the previous chapter, science is demonstrating how our minds can experience *trans-locality* through telepathy, extrasensory perception, and clairaudience. Experiences that once belonged to mystics and shamans are now being replicated in the laboratories of the world. As challenging as this might be to some, we now know that each of us, using the power of our subconscious mind, can connect to transcendence and work wonders every day.

> *Please remember: Our life is the canvas upon which we can paint a masterpiece using the power of the subconscious mind. By understanding its power to store experiences and craft them together into a life script, we can use that same power to change our internal programming and live in a new way.*

Putting It All Together

I started our exploration of the human mind with a brief look at the power and reliability of the conscious mind. Thanks to the conscious mind, we can reason, make decisions, analyze, and exercise our willpower. We saw that as twenty-first century people, our education has been largely focused on creating the strongest conscious mind that we could—sometimes to the neglect of our deep inner selves. One author has gone so far as to say that the people of the Middle Ages, with their emphasis on religious symbolism and ritual, were much more in tune with the subconscious mind than we are today.

We learned that 10 percent of the mind's power is used by the conscious mind, which explains why consistent life changes and personal transformation are so difficult for most of us. We can decide to change, and those of us with the willpower of a Hercules can keep at it for a long time. But ultimately, using the power of the conscious mind to change a long-held habit, pattern, or belief is as ineffective as trying to power our car with the AAA batteries of our flashlight. You might get enough juice to turn on the radio, but you won't get much further.

Only when we understand how the subconscious mind works and then put that understanding into action can we make the changes we desire. Using the power of the subconscious mind to create new emotional patterns, such as hope, positivity, love, and emotional resilience, we release untapped energy and connect ourselves to a greater mind. This is part of your birthright, or to use more modern language, it's part of the hardware of your personal computer. It's who you are!

So, from here, you are going to learn how to use your entire mind so you can prosper, thrive, and have fun doing it. When clients first come into my hypnotherapy office, I explain a little bit about their mind and how hypnosis works. At the end of the introduction, I tell them, "To make the change you want, you'll work with the 10 percent of your conscious mind, and I'll work with the 90 percent of your subconscious mind, and together we'll work wonders." This usually evokes a smile because by the time people come to me, they've struggled on their own unsuccessfully to make change. When they see how and why the change can happen through our partnership, they are relieved and excited to get to work.

The first lesson they learn is this: *while the subconscious mind holds most of the power, it needs the conscious mind to put it to work*. After all I've said about the recording and projecting power of the subconscious, this might seem a bit counterintuitive, but to live the kind of life that

I believe you want to live, you will need to have the active engagement of the conscious mind.

In his book *The Power of the Subconscious Mind*, Joseph Murphy wrote:

> The captain is the master of the ship; his orders are followed out; likewise, your conscious mind is the captain, the master of your ship. Your body and all of your affairs represent the ship. Your subconscious mind takes the orders you give it based upon your belief and suggestions accepted as true.

You can probably imagine any number of metaphors to illustrate this point. From the conductor guiding an orchestra to the NFL coach leading a team, the conscious mind has the power through laser-like focus to communicate with the subconscious to get astounding results. After all, you've lived your entire life using the power of the conscious mind to do incredible things, so let's learn how to use *all* your mind to create a new you. The subconscious is ready and waiting; all it needs is your focus, commitment, and passion. Let's start that process now.

Summary

As we have continued our introduction into the power of our magnificent mind, we've come to see some characteristics of the subconscious mind that both give it its power and make it a challenge to work with. We've discovered that the subconscious mind is always alert and active; records every event; uses symbolic language to communicate with us; processes information literally; and thinks only in the present moment, creating reality out of our programming. By properly understanding and interacting with our magnificent mind, we can create the masterpiece of our lives.

CHAPTER 5

THE FORMULA TO SUCCESS

What the mind of man can conceive and believe, it can achieve.

—Napoleon Hill

One of the things I loved about being a detective was the challenge of putting together all the available clues and evidence to "make the case." From physical evidence like fingerprints and blood spatters to sorting through the often-contradictory statements of victims, witness, and suspects, my job was to see the whole picture and present a case to the prosecutor that could be taken to trial. Sometimes the task was simple (thanks to video cameras), and at other times it was laborious and took days—if not weeks or even months—to put the puzzle together.

Fortunately, for our work together, making powerful and lasting change is simple. By the time you have successfully done what you set out to do, you will feel deep satisfaction and joy. But there might be just a tinge of frustration at the trail's end. *Why*, you might wonder, *were these simple and transformative skills not taught in every school in the land?* How many times did you sit in a classroom and wonder what the real world had to do with the subjects being taught? Well, here is a method to make optimal change that is direct, tangible, powerful, and tested in the lives of real people every day.

The simplicity of this method is stunning; but in the beginning, it may not seem all that easy. We are, after all, talking about learning to use your mind in a new way, and we've seen how repetitive patterns of thinking and feeling are embedded in your subconscious mind. So, creating the "new mind" requires diligence, concentration, imagination, excitement, and gratitude. For many, this is not an easy combination to bring together in the mind. But don't worry. Thousands of people have discovered the magic, and so can you.

The Power of State

Ever since I was a little boy, I have loved helicopters and have always wanted to fly one. In my hometown, there was a commuter heliport where, for several years, a helicopter company flew shuttle service to the Los Angeles International Airport for a hefty fee. I remember riding my bicycle down to the heliport and sitting transfixed as the helicopters arrived, hovered, landed, took on passengers, and then took off. Sometimes I was so moved by watching the helicopters flying, I sat on my bike and cried like a baby. When I was a police sergeant, I flew as an observer in helicopters to learn tactics that would assist me in directing my officers on the ground. Truth be told, I just love flying in helicopters, so I get into one every chance I have.

I've made obtaining my helicopter pilot's license a goal and have made friends with an army helicopter pilot who told me some of the tricks of the trade. When you fly a helicopter, you must concern yourselves with many instruments and techniques to get you and keep you airborne. My pilot friend told me that learning to fly a helicopter is very different from learning to fly a fix-winged aircraft. He said that you must use your body in a way that a 747 pilot would never understand, and you must be a very instinctual flyer.

For our purposes, though, the point is that to fly a helicopter successfully, you must know every technology and technique to safely and successfully enjoy your flight. The same is true for us as we undertake the journey of making powerful and massive change. We should understand how the process works and why, and then apply it with an attention rivaling that of a novice helicopter pilot.

In the chapters on the subconscious mind, I pointed out that whenever we experience something that our brain is familiar with, we enter a state of mind that is a combination of automatic thinking and feeling. Thanks to the associations and identifications in our subconscious mind, just thinking about food can trigger a whole array of feelings and emotions operating at the same time, which we call a "state." If the thought of your favorite sports team causes pleasure to course through your body, in that moment you are experiencing a state. The thoughts of a romantic encounter can also elevate your emotions and anticipatory sensations and put you in a state before you even reach the place where your date awaits.

Again, what is true of positive states is true also of negative ones. If your subconscious programming is such that you experienced crushing anxiety in school, the mere thought of going back for a graduate degree can induce a state that keeps you from even filling out the application. When you think about sitting in a classroom again, your heart begins to beat more rapidly, your skin gets clammy, and your muscles seem ready to snap. This is because you are in a state, and it is overwhelming your ability to think logically—that is, with the conscious mind.

So, the first step to using your mind to lose weight, stop smoking, heal negative relationship patterns, make a million dollars, or cure yourself from cancer is to become aware of how you experience "state." I guarantee that each time you try to make a change and are unsuccessful, your body has run through a series of states. When you first decide to make a change in your life, you likely experienced a hopeful state. You told yourself why you needed to make the change, and you might even have visualized yourself realizing your goal. Your emotional state then encourages you to launch your endeavor. Then, when the going got tough, your body enters a state of thinking and feeling that is in line with your subconscious programming.

Some people *love* challenges, so their emotions and physiology respond very differently from that of the person who is terrified of change. This intermediate state would either propel you on or drag you down. Ultimately, though, when the task at hand seems unmanageable or the goal you want to achieve appears unreachable, your mind puts you into a state that signals defeat to you, and you quit.

Remember that one of the primary roles of the subconscious mind is to regulate all your physical, emotional, and psychological systems, so when the challenge that you face seems too great, the subconscious immediately flips the override switch, and your motivation and ability levels drop through the floor. What makes this so frustrating for us is that, although the subconscious management of our thoughts and feelings is natural, we are not a victim of an objective reality but of the programming of our life scripts.

For example, you may set out to run a marathon and start training for it. You have watched so many marathon races, sometimes even going to a race and standing at the finish line to cheer on the winners. You see how hard work and dedication pay off, and you are in an excited and hopeful state of mind. Day after day, you get up before work, lace on your running shoes, and head out to run before getting ready to work. Some days are easier than others, and your iPhone race timer tells you that you are making slow but steady progress.

But then you run into a challenge that you hadn't expected. No matter how hard you train, there will come a time when you reach a performance plateau, and for a while you quit making progress. Sports experts tell us this. They teach that if you can just keep training while running *across* the plateau, eventually your inner systems will adapt, and you will improve your performance again.

And this is where your state comes in. Depending on your ability to tolerate frustration, you might feel that this task is too daunting, and so you quit. If you examine your conditioned thought patterns and subconscious programming in other areas of your life, you might see that you have a history of quitting when a task seems overwhelming. But please remember, this isn't because you are a weak or bad person. These patterns of surrender are the subconscious mind's way of protecting you based on what has been programmed within, and it protects you by creating a state that pulls the plug on your energy and emotions.

Homeo-what?

In hypnotherapy training, we are taught that this powerful but programmed resistance to change is called *homeostasis*. Homeostasis—literally "return to the one"—is defined by Dictionary.com as "the tendency of the body to seek and maintain a condition of balance or equilibrium within its internal environment, even when faced with external changes." Biologists have long known that the body has a "set point," and when it is threatened by some external challenge or threat, it uses all its considerable energy to return to its original state. The most obvious example of this is your body temperature. For most of us, the norm is 98.6 degrees, yet it fluctuates according to the body's needs. But ultimately it returns to your norm, and you are in good health again.

Homeostasis is a reality of our emotional systems as well, and you must understand it and take this into consideration in your journey of transformation. For example, you may want to release substantial weight from your body, but your subconscious mind has been programmed to believe that those extra pounds are part of the shield by which you protect yourself from vulnerability and intimacy. So, as the weight starts to come off, you find yourself feeling anxious, moody, irritable, and generally no fun to be around. This is homeostasis in action. It's as though your subconscious is saying, "Warning, change is scary. Avoid at all costs." Without the support of the transformed mind, the subconscious impulse to self-correct makes changing your body image and weight management very difficult.

The Necessity of State Shifting

To become a master at transformation, you should become very familiar with how your thinking and feeling creates a state. No matter how hard you want to make a change, if your subconscious feels threatened and activates the homeostasis switch, you're going nowhere fast. Thankfully, however, I am going to show you how to override homeostasis and write new code for your powerful subconscious mind.

1. Are you and your feelings on a first-name basis?

The first step is to become aware of how you are feeling in any given moment. This may seem both simple and obvious, but for many of us, it's a challenge. We thunder through our day and consciously become aware of our feelings only when they are on red alert. We come home exhausted although our body has been pointing to growing fatigue all day long. We awaken in the middle of the night with terrible heartburn. But if we were a bit more honest with ourselves, we'd recognize that we've been anxious about a conflict with a coworker for weeks. Or maybe it isn't until our third tequila shot that we recognize how stressed out we've been.

To access the mind-states necessary to make powerful change, you must be able to tell in a moment how you are feeling because the feeling state, when coupled with relaxation and imagination, will work wonders. To begin to feel can be harder than you think (pun intended). So, shut the door to the room that you're in, turn off the phone (you can do it; I believe in you), and let's practice feeling your state right now. If you're listening to this as an audiobook, let me lead you through the exercise, but if you are reading this, record it on your phone or some other device so you can experience it fully.

Coming Home to Yourself—A Meditation

First, sit in a very comfortable chair. Being a hypnotherapist, I prefer a recliner, but comfort and support are all that's needed for this exercise.

Next, close your eyes and begin to breathe gently through your nose. Don't force the breath; just be aware of how it effortlessly flows in and out of your nose. Feel the temperature of the air as you breathe in and out.

Now, with your eyes closed and your simple breath flowing through your nose, feel your feet from the inside out. Feel free to wiggle your toes if you must, but feel your feet as they rest on the floor. Are you wearing shoes? Feel those. Are you in your stocking feet? Feel the fabric of surrounding your feet. Are your feet bare? Feel the air around your feet.

Now, as your eyes are stilled closed and your breath constant and even, feel your lower legs and your knees. Can you feel your shins and your calves? Can you feel your kneecaps and the backs of your knees? Are you wearing pants or a skirt, or are your legs bare? Feel your knees as they are attached to your shins.

Now feel your thighs and your hamstrings. Feel as they brush up against whatever you are wearing, and again become aware of your breath. Feel how your legs rest against your chair and what that feels like.

With your eyes closed, feel what yoga teachers call your "sitting bones." Feel how your whole body supports you as you sit in this moment. With your eyes closed and your simple breath flowing, allow yourself to feel "sitting."

Now feel your lower back and your stomach. Feel how your stomach rises and falls as you enjoy the simple act of breathing. Feel your solar plexus area and your mid-back. Can you feel your spine as you continue to breathe in and out through your nose with your eyes closed?

Now feel your chest, and see if you can feel your heart beat. Can you feel how your lungs open slightly with the in-breath and close with the out-breath? Feel your trapezius muscles and how they wrap around your shoulders.

With your eyes still gently closed and your breath even and balanced, feel you neck and your throat. Can you feel your neck supporting your head? Can you feel the air you breathe traveling down your throat?

Next feel your head. You are already aware of your eyes and nose, so try to feel your lips, your jaws, and your ears. Can you feel your forehead and the back of your head? Can you feel the top of your head?

Now, with your eyes still closed and your breath flowing gently, feel your entire body from the top of your head down to the bottom of your feet. Make it like a scan where you feel your body completely and yet become aware of its parts as well.

Finally, feel your psychological and emotional state. Keep focusing on your closed eyes and the breath at your nose, but try to feel how you are "feeling" right now. Are you happy? Anxious? Confused? Satisfied? Intrigued? Hopeful? There are hundreds of emotional combinations to feel, but just try in this moment to feel what is "live" for you right now.

As you end this exploration, notice how relaxed you feel. Take a deep breath, and when you exhale, open your eyes.

How was that experience for you? Was it hit-and-miss, or were you amazed at how much sensation you could feel. As I said earlier, this is the first step toward mastery because if we don't know how we feel in any given moment, we can't make the state changes necessary to download new subconscious patterns.

If this was a difficult exercise for you, make the commitment to practice it at least once a day in its entirety. You can also spot-check yourself by becoming aware of how you feel physically and emotionally at different times of the day. When you stop at red lights, do a quick scan, and feel what's going on. Or set your alarm on your phone to beep every ninety minutes or so, and take a nice deep breath and check in with how you feel. Like every skill, practice makes the master, so the better you become at being aware of your state, the quicker we move on to the next step.

Flight, Flight, or Freeze

The next step on the journey to transforming the subconscious mind is understanding how we relate to fear or threat. I grew up in a police family, became a scout in police organizations, served as a military policeman in the army, and became a civilian cop. Among my other accomplishments is becoming a defensive tactics instructor with a black belt.

Never in all that time, in those various versions of my chosen profession, did I have a class in understanding fear. This was too bad because over the course of that career, I was hit, kicked, shot at, bitten, and stabbed. I had to storm an apartment to rescue hostages and go into burning buildings to help people escape sure death. In other words, there were plenty of times that I was terrified, but nobody taught us what to do with the very real fear we were feeling.

Fear is a natural response to a threat, but in my police culture, only weaklings (that's the only printable word I could use here) were afraid. After harrowing experiences, we would tell each other that it was "only adrenaline" and it would pass. But like I said previously, the master of transformation can't be afraid of the fear response.

One of the crazy things about life is that we are often as afraid of success as we are of failure because both represent change that can be uncomfortable to our established way of life. Therefore, we must come to understand it for what it is and release it when it has served its purpose.

We know that the ability to use fear to our advantage is an evolutionary skill handed down from our ancient ancestors. When three

53

of them were hunting for something to eat and encountered a wooly mammoth, an instinctual set of physiological/emotional responses kicked in. If our first intrepid hunter thought he might be able to kill the animal and feed his family for a year, he would use the fear energy to attack. If the second, one of the smartest of his tribe, knew that anything else might be less satisfying, but in the end, he might live longer, he would use the fear energy to flee. And if the third was the hapless one of the family, he might be so overtaken with fear that he could neither fight nor flee, and so he froze, hoping to blend in and be ignored.

Regardless of outcome, all three hunters were undergoing rapid and powerful biological changes to enable them to fight, run, or try to become invisible. Their heart started pumping faster, their digestion slowed down, their breathing pattern became more effective, and they developed tunnel vision to see either their prey or their escape route better. (Kind of like how you react before getting on stage to make that presentation before everyone?)

Understanding Your Nervous System

Our trio of hunters demonstrated for us a function of our central nervous system that we need to become aware of if we are to make lasting change. Within our autonomic (automatic) nervous system, two functions help the body maintain equilibrium according the circumstance of the moment: the sympathetic nervous and the parasympathetic nervous systems. Both are continually operating in our bodies to some degree, and our job in transformation is to dial one up and scale the other back.

1. The sympathetic nervous system

The sympathetic nervous system is the part of our autonomic nervous system that facilitates the changes in our bodily function that help us survive a moment of crisis or peril. This largely happens through the release of norepinephrine and epinephrine, which creates what we commonly call an adrenaline rush. When the sympathetic nervous system is activated, our heart rate increases, glucose is released to provide more energy, our airways widen to increase oxygen supplies to the body, our pupils dilate to sharpen our field of vision, our digestive activity slows down to conserve energy, and our bladder relaxes to get rid of excess weight that my slow us down.

So, the sympathetic nervous system accelerates some bodily functions while it suppresses others. This explains why the night that I was on gang suppression patrol and a sniper shot out the back window of my police car, I "automatically" stepped on the gas, got out of the line of fire, then jumped from my still moving car, took a position of protection, and pulled out my gun while calling for help. The recording of my radio transmission didn't sound like my voice at all—and in some ways, it wasn't; it was my evolutionary ancestor who was reporting for duty while trying to decide whether to fight, flee, or freeze. I had instantly broken out in a sweat, was shaking like I had a fever, and (yes, I must admit) had wet my pants.

Since creativity requires the ability to think beyond the present moment and to tap into inner resources of abundance, a state of anxiety is going to limit the ways you can interact with the world. If you are fighting for your life with a woolly mammoth, you aren't likely going to be able to envision a new algorithm or hear a new symphony in the depth of your soul. You are going to be focused on getting as far away from the threat as you think is possible.

Living as we do in what has come to be called the Age of Anxiety, our sympathetic nervous systems are more active than many of us are aware of. An article recently on the Daily Beast news site pointed out that college admissions professionals in America have noticed a sharp uptick in students with generalized and specific anxiety disorders. Using what researchers call a longitudinal study, they discovered that the stressed-out kids coming to college today were born after the attacks of

9/11. For these students, the attacks of that day and the heightened sense of insecurity that has blanketed the United States since have created life scripts in their subconscious mind of anxiety and fear.

I finished this book after the presidential election of 2016 was decided and have been amazed at both the fear and the loathing that seemed to grip our nation in the days after the results were announced.

I'm sure you can see the implications of fear for our work together. While the sympathetic nervous response is great when dealing with woolly mammoths or gang snipers, it blocks one's ability to think new thoughts and to trust emerging patterns of belief. As we'll see shortly, rewriting subconscious programs is most effective when done from a place of deep relaxation—in order words, not when we are under the spell of the sympathetic nervous system.

Our fears and the activation of the sympathetic nervous response need not be in the in-the-moment, life-threatening category. I once worked with a client who was making wonderful progress in becoming the man he wanted to be, but in one of our sessions he froze up on me. He started to hyperventilate and broke out in a sweat as his muscles began to twitch like he was being jolted with electricity. We discovered that we had just touched on an old and deep pattern in his subconscious mind—that his job was to be a "good boy" or he would be punished violently. In that moment, he had collapsed into part of his life script, and his state had changed in an instant. He became a little boy again, and even his voice took on a childlike character to it. So we had to walk him through a journey of forgiving his father and introduce a new subconscious pattern of support before we could continue to move him toward his dream self.

2. The parasympathetic nervous system

If the sympathetic nervous system rings all the alarms and supercharges the body's response to threat, the parasympathetic nervous system is just the opposite. Biologists call it the "rest and digest" or "feed and breed" part of the nervous system. Where the sympathetic system releases norepinephrine and epinephrine in the body, the parasympathetic enables relaxation responses to flourish, increasing peace of mind and the relaxation of all the systems that had been ramped up in fight, flight, or freeze.

As with the client from the example above, sometimes it's necessary to feel the fear that lurks just under the surface of consciousness, release it, and activate the parasympathetic response. It is from a state of rest and peacefulness that deep creativity and the pump of transformation is primed. In the next chapter, we're going to practice inducing this state of peaceful, focused concentration, and from there we'll activate deep and lasting change.

Let's reflect together:

Please answer these questions as honestly you can. Nobody will ever see the answer but you, so honesty is the best policy.

What would you say your baseline emotional state is day to day? Are you a fearful person? When you do feel fear, and where in your body do you feel it? Of what are you the most afraid?

_____

_____

_____

_____

_____

_____

_____

_____

Summary

As we continue to fine-tune our understanding of our magnificent mind, we've learned that to make change successfully, we need to work with both our neurology and our automatic physical processes. We discussed the power of our state of mind and have seen how it is a combination of both learned emotional and physical responses to our perceived circumstances. We saw how important it is to be able to change our state in a way that will support our desire to change.

We learned about the power of homeostasis, our built-in self-regulating system, and how it affects us not only physically but emotionally and psychologically as well. One of the prime examples of the interaction between mind and body is the fight, flight, or freeze reaction to perceived danger and stress. We looked at why our mind and body reacts differently to danger than to love, and we saw how creativity is blocked by fear, worry, and anxiety.

CHAPTER 6

SUCCESS WITH THE MAGNIFICENT MIND

Success or failure depends more upon attitude than upon capacity; successful men act as though they have accomplished or are enjoying something. Soon it becomes a reality. Act, look, feel successful, conduct yourself accordingly, and you will be amazed at the positive results.

—*William James*

I once read a novel whose message stayed with me long after I forgot its name and author. I suppose it falls in the "Indiana Jones saves the world" genre of storytelling. It was set in contemporary times in the Middle East, and the two heroes, a man and a woman, were forced into a search for a secret formula that would keep civilization from being destroyed. They were chased by villains and soldiers of fortune from Rome to Athens, to Istanbul, and finally to Cypress, where the formula was discovered and the day was saved. What I particularly remember about this story was a discovery they made along the way.

In the barren landscape between Ephesus and Istanbul, they were desperate to hide from their pursuers, and they discovered what looked like a fox's den. Small and dark, it didn't seem to offer much protection, but they decided to both squeeze in there to avoid capture. Once they were wedged in, their weight against the back of the space caused built-up debris and sediment to give way, and they found an unlit passage that led somewhere away from the surface. With seemingly nothing to lose, they groped their way down a narrow path, encountering all sorts of bugs and slimy crawling things.

The further underground they went, the less oxygen they had, and soon they were at a crisis point. Do they stay where they were, in darkness and with little air to breathe, or do they make their way back to the surface in the hopes that the bad guys were long gone? After a hushed but heated argument, they agreed to descend further in hopes of finding a way to the surface where their hunters couldn't find them.

As soon as they made the decision to move on, the ground underneath them gave way, and (in true Indiana Jones fashion) they slid for hundreds of yards and despaired of life as they went further and faster than they could control. Like all adventures that favor the hero, their slide ended, and they found themselves in the largest cave that they had ever seen. This cave was so big that it housed an underground city. Light seemed to emanate from the walls of the cave, and a crystal river flowed alongside the remarkable city.

While they were astonished with their discovery, they were unsure what to do because they didn't know if those cave dwellers would be friendly to them. But they had no choice but to proceed into the city, where they were greeted by spectacular beings. While human, each of the men and women of the city were radiant and very welcoming.

Our heroes were fascinated that the buildings in the city were made of a crystalline marble, and the decorations and appointments were made of gold, silver, and precious jewels. They discovered that the inhabitants of this magical place had once been surface dwellers. But after years of purification and effort, they had been welcomed by the elders and were transformed into beautiful, immortal beings. They possessed infinite wisdom and power and could create and transform with merely a thought.

Of course, they held the key to finding the world-saving secret that our duo was looking for, but they also offered that they stay in that wondrous place and become luminous beings themselves. Much to the reader's relief, our intrepid heroes chose to return to the surface with the secret knowledge, and—viola—the world was saved once again.

I took the time to recount this story because it illustrates the process and power of your transformation. For most of your life, you have been on the hero's journey, trying to find success, purpose, health, and passion. You've learned and experienced much, but you've been pursued by the thieves of fear, doubt, frustration, and despair. You've heard about the power of your mind to change your life, and now you've discovered that it's in the eternal depths of your subconscious mind that you will find the power to make your dreams come true. So now we'll begin our journey "underground" to the luminous city of your deep mind and discover the power that awaits your return.

A Word about the Process

My purpose in writing this book has been to introduce you to the marvels of your magnificent mind. Starting with an overview of your mind's power and its ability to change your life, you've seen concrete examples of its wonderworking power. Then you had a crash course in how your mind works, and you saw how its dynamic patterns and energies are at the service of your transformation. Now, as you take steps to understand and apply this method of reprogramming your subconscious, you will begin to see changes in your life.

To help you in this adventure, I want to offer you four gifts. If understood and used effectively, they will speed up your success, and you can enjoy the process along the way.

1. The Gift of Clarity

The first gift is the gift of clarity. For this process to be most effective and for you to see results quickly, you need to be crystal clear about your goals and objectives. My own coach, Jodi Nicholson, reminds me at times of a drill instructor as she forever drills the words "clarity, clarity, clarity" into me as I work with her. Her point is well taken; arriving at clarity about our goals focuses the powers of our mind in a way that nothing else will.

In an interview, fashion designer Diane von Furstenberg shared one of her principles of success when she said, "Clarity is the most important thing. I can compare clarity to pruning in gardening. You know, you need to be clear. If you are not clear, nothing is going to happen." Clarity is the process of eliminating paralyzing options and aligning with your most important values. Very often we *think* we know what we want, but when we go through the process of clarifying our goals, we see a lot of emotional clutter in the way.

For example, many people who want to be successful have only a vague clue as to why. When you ask them what success would bring, very often the answer is "lots of money" or "fame and notoriety" or "professional acclaim." But when you work to clarify, they discover that what they want are feelings of safety, security, love, meaning, purpose, or the ability to contribute on a massive scale. So, as their idea of success becomes clearer, people either discover new ways to sustain the feeling state that they want, or they get new insight into how to achieve their goals.

The process of clarifying your goals through developing a crystal-clear vision of where you want to go is foundational in business and career planning, but when programming changes into the subconscious mind, it becomes even more important. Remember, the subconscious mind records *everything,* and the more a particular thought or energy pattern is recorded, the stronger it becomes until it is assimilated into your life script. So, to have a transformative impact on your subconscious mind, you must be certain what you want because you are going to use your laser-like power of focused attention, intention, repetition, and emotion to launch the new program.

As mentioned in chapter 2, Dr. Joe Dispenza said that people who recovered from "incurable" disease developed such clarity about what their healed body would feel like that they were then able to use that clarity to drive the change home into their subconscious mind. So, the first essential step in transformation is to know what you want and why. Motivation plays a huge role in making massive change, so the clearer you are on the why, the better chance that your subconscious will provide you all the support necessary to succeed.

Clarity in Action: What Do You Want?

You've come to this book with an idea about what change you'd like to make. Whether it is financial or professional success, new and improved relationships, releasing a bad habit, or anything else, we always start at the same place. Take some time to become calm and relaxed, perhaps using the breathing techniques with your eyes closed that we used before. Then ask yourself these questions:

What do you really want to change about your life?

_____

_____

_____

_____

_____

Why do you want to make this change? (The more specific you can be here, the better. Pay attention to any feelings that come up when you answer the question, and write them down.)

_____

_____

Have you tried to change this before? What happened? Were you able to see some change for a while, or was it a no-go from the onset. How did it feel then, and how does the memory feel now?

What will the quality of your life be if you don't make this change now? (Again, in addition to the logical answer that your mind serves up, notice the feeling state that arises when you think about remaining stuck where you are.)

Have you achieved a greater sense of clarity about the transformation that you'd like to see? If so, it's time to take the next step and discover the second gift.

2. The Gift of Intention

Your second gift is understanding the power of intention. Once you have the "what" and "why" of your desired change, you can take the first mental action step to accomplishing it. Your ability to be determined to see this process to its successful completion—no matter what—is what I call the power of intention. It's in this vein that Wayne Dyer said, "Your intention creates your reality." The power of your intention constructs a shelter around your dream until the day that it bursts forth from the subconscious mind into your daily life.

This power of intention has been known for millennia. The Upanishads, some of the most ancient Hindu texts, puts it this way: "You are what your deep, driving desire is. As your desire is, so is your will. As your will is, so is your deed. As your deed is, so is your destiny." In other words, your intention reveals where your commitments are. Because of your love for your family, you may arise before the sun, commute in horrible traffic, and sit in a cubicle for hours, working on projects that bore you. You wish you could do something else (which I am going to help you with), but you do it because it seems the best way to fulfill your commitment to your family. When Jesus said in the New Testament, "Where your treasure is, there you'll find your heart," he was talking about the power of your intention and commitment to what you value.

When I lead men's retreats, we spend a couple of hours on the power of their intention. I tell them to look at both their checkbook and calendar (C&C) to discover the power of their intention. This exercise shows the men what they value in "real time" is, and from there they can adjust their energies as necessary. If they say that their family is their number-one priority but their C&C shows that they spend little time or money on their family, we know what's out of alignment: their intention or execution. And then, with the gift of clarity, they can realign themselves to their intention.

So, in personal transformation work, once we have the "what we want" down as well as the "why we want it," we set our intention to bring it to pass. The methods and techniques I teach are simple and powerful, but they take a commitment to regular, sustained practice. Remember, the subconscious mind cannot be tricked; it takes you at your word. So, if you make the intention in your conscious mind that you will do the work, no matter what resistance arises, it agrees to the partnership—and the fun begins.

Intention in Action: The Contract of Transformation

Please write out in your own words your intention to change. This may seem a little simplistic, but when dealing with the subconscious mind, you need to build cognitive pillars to allow the change to happen. I am going to ask you to spend at least twenty minutes, twice a day, practicing the techniques you are learning. This amount of time seems to be a good minimum to launch the program of change. So, if you are willing to do whatever it takes, write it out in your contract.

Use bold, absolute language in your contract with yourself. The subconscious responds to feelings, metaphors, and images. You are going to get very used to strong emotions in the service of change quickly, so reach for the stars here. Make your statement of intent below, sign it, date it, and then celebrate by doing something that makes you feel positive and happy.

---

3. The Gift of Release

Remember the story about the man whose subconscious mind activated a pattern of fear around his father's disapproval. In childhood, being a "bad boy" resulted in severe punishment, so his subconscious mind created an association that essentially said, "Be a good boy or you'll die." Using the power of hypnosis and neuro-linguistic programming, we allowed my client to feel the fear of impending death and then to release the energy to let it pass. Only with the successful repetition of recalling the association, allowing the energy of the fear to rise, and then learning to pass it was the client able to regain the improvement that he had been making.

In transformative work, it's important to understand the role of emotions as energy. All too often we think that emotions are somehow part of our emotional and psychological structure, when they are what John Bradshaw called energy in motion. Emotions are a felt response to an experience or perception that then releases an energetic discharge in our body.

In 1972, Dr. Paul Eckman studied cultures all around the world and concluded that there are six basic emotions known to humankind. He felt that fear, disgust, anger, surprise, happiness, and sadness were the primary emotions that everyone has, regardless of culture or religious training. In the 1980s, Robert Plutchik suggested that there were eight emotional combinations, which he called the Wheel of Emotions. He concluded that emotions can be combined to make new emotions and that these emotions create "master emotions" in the human experience.

The gift of release, as we are going to use it here, suggests that (1) all emotions are energy, (2) all emotions are merely energy seeking release, (3) some emotions affect us so strongly that they become part of our subconscious programming, and (4) by learning to recognize, name, feel, and then release emotions, we can become free of their destructive influence. This process (and it is a process) can allow you to feel deep emotions in healthy ways, engage them, and release them.

I am indebted to Lester Levinson, who founded the Sedona Method in 1952, and Larry Crane, who refined the Sedona Method into what has come to be known as the Release Technique. Both men have experienced radical healings themselves and have taught thousands of others how to dramatically change every area of the lives by understanding the proper role of emotions.

Imagine that a strong emotion is like an ocean wave that crashes onto a beach. What does it do next? Gravity pulls the dispersed water back into the ocean for the next round of waves making their way back to shore. What would happen if just before the wave crashed onto the beach, we dropped a *huge* cement box around part of the wave? What would happen? All the energy of the wave would be absorbed inside the box, and its natural rhythm would be disrupted. Yet the moment we removed the cement structure, the water would return to the natural cycle of the ocean, and balance is restored.

The same is true of our emotional life. If we can view emotions as waves of energy whose purpose is to manifest and then return to the ocean of consciousness, we will be less inclined either to hold onto them or to block their expression. In this work, there will be times when, like the client referred to above, emotions surface. Perhaps they are tied to some potent event in our memory, or maybe they show up because we are "just emotional people." (The most common emotions seem to be fear and anger.) Rather than let the emotion embody itself and create discomfort or block your progress, you'll learn to acknowledge it and let it go.

Becoming proficient in this process takes work because we have not been trained to interact with our emotions this way. Many people either stuff away their emotions, and they gain negative strength and cause a whole host of physical and psychological problems, or they "let fly" with their emotions, consequences be damned. The method of release allows us to familiarize ourselves with the power of our emotions, not fear them, and allow them to dissipate on their own. In the final chapter, where we practice transformation, we'll work a bit at allowing emotions to rise, integrate them into the moment, and let them go. This is very important because without it, we will get stuck and not able to make the change we want.

It's also important to be able to work with our emotions because we are going to use them to drive the change that we want to bring to the subconscious. So the more comfortable you are with emotion, the stronger your work will be.

Release in Action: Explore Your Emotional Program

As with the previous exercises, take a minute to become calm and reflective. Then look back over your personal emotional history and answer this question: When confronted with emotions, I usually _____.
Do you suppress emotions, express them, or blast others? Again, be honest, since only you will see your answer.

What do you feel as you look at your emotional profile? Sometimes people feel shame or weakness? There are no right or wrong answers here. Just get to know yourself as fully as you can.

_____

_____

_____

_____

_____

_____

_____

4. The Gift of Imagination

The final gift that will enable you to master your transformation is the gift of imagination. Imagination is in some ways the primary driver of personal change. Regardless of what you want to accomplish in this work, imagination is the royal road to getting you there. Playwright and author George Bernard Shaw once said that imagination is the "beginning of creation. You imagine what you desire, you will what you imagine and at last you create what you will." In hypnosis, we create a state where your mind accepts the most powerful idea presented to it (your desired change), and then we use imagination as its vehicle to create it.

Given that the subconscious mind primarily interacts with symbols, images, metaphors, and feelings, you can understand why the stronger your imagination, the more powerful your transformation will be. When you visualize yourself as a nonsmoker on a consistent, sustained basis, and you fuel that imagination with strong, positive emotion and remove emotional blocks to becoming an "air breather," the day comes when the desire to smoke leaves, never to return.

The same can be true about the process of manifesting health, wealth, and success: for powerful change to become real, your imagination must implant the image of your desire strongly in your subconscious mind until that is the only idea there is. Dr. Joseph Murphy says the subconscious always accepts the stronger of two ideas, and the imagination always wins out over repetitive thought if it is strong enough.

Every wonder was once an idea in someone's fertile imagination. From the Eiffel Tower to the Space Shuttle to a gourmet meal, everything was conceived by the gift of imagination. Dr. Martin Luther King, Mahatma Gandhi, Halle Berry, George Frederic Handel, and Bill Gates all had at least one thing in common: they could see a future yet unrealized and use the power of their mind to bring it to pass.

The truth is, you've had an active imagination all your life. How can I say that without knowing you? Just look at your life as it is today; it reflects the images and stories that you've told yourself about reality to this point. At some subconscious level, you've imagined every lack and limitation that is in your life, and your mind has agreed to make it real for you. So now we are going to flip the switch and put your imagination to work for you. Your future vision of success in all your endeavors begins in the imaginative power of your subconscious mind, so boldly embrace it, and put it to work for you today.

Imagination in Action: Paint a Portrait of Your Future

Now is the time to get excited about what lies before you. So let's have some fun with this exercise. Take a moment, as always, to get calm and settled, and then put pen to paper. In the space below, imagine the most fantastic version of the life you want to have.

Visualize the personal power you'll experience when you meet your goals. See your loved ones congratulating you and telling you how proud they are of you. Describe in depth the benefits you will bring to your world, and begin to feel joy as you write these words.

Give free rein to your imagination. Fly, laugh, dance, create, love, prosper— and have fun!

Summary

In this chapter, we reviewed four gifts that we can give ourselves as we begin the process of letting our magnificent mind work for us. We saw how clarity, intention, release, and imagination are all vital components in setting the stage for the transformative journey. Each of these four gifts is worth its weight in gold individually, but when put together, they deliver a knockout blow to resistance and fear. They are the culmination of thousands of years of spiritual and personal development, so let's become as proficient as we can and deepen our pool of receptivity to powerful change.

CHAPTER 7

A NEW YOU

As a single footstep will not make a path on the earth,
so a single thought will not make a pathway in the mind.
To make a deep physical path, we walk again and again.
To make a deep mental path, we must think over and over
the kind of thoughts we wish to dominate our lives.

—*Henry David Thoreau*

People love how-to programs today. From the seven steps to this or the twelve steps of that, we love practical, no-nonsense ways to accomplish our goals, especially if there is a Caribbean cruise involved. In our fast-paced day and age, we want to pick up helpful tips that maximize our good without getting us bogged down in details. I've crafted this book to do a little of both; I've provided you with an introduction to your magnificent mind, shown you the possibilities of what it can do, and offered a way to use it to realize your dreams.

If you come away from this thinking that all you need to do is adopt a new technique or learn a new skill, I've failed you because the process of changing your life is just that: changing your life. A dictionary definition of transformation is "a thorough or dramatic change in form

73

or appearance." In other words, to transform is to make new. Einstein once said, "We cannot solve our problems with the same consciousness that created them." We can't become prosperous by maintaining a poverty consciousness any more than we can learn to swim by staying out of the pool.

To allow powerful change to happen, you must create new pathways of thought, new perceptions of reality, and a new sense of who you are as a person. Smokers must become nonsmokers in their minds long before they kick the habit, and paupers must become wealthy in their minds before experiencing abundance in the outer world.

The Center for Integrated Healing in Canada lists ten traits that are common to people who spontaneously recover from incurable disease.

1. Despite being told that their cancer is incurable, they have a deep belief that their body can heal itself.
2. They take control and assume a recovery program that is unique to them. They reclaim their own responsibility rather than solely relying on experts.
3. They reconnect with spirit, awakening long hidden desires and aspirations.
4. They deepen and bring honesty to their relationships with others.
5. A compete reassessment of their lives is undertaken. They are willing to change lifestyle, career, goals, and relationships.
6. They change their diet to include decreasing processed, refined foods and animal fats and consuming more fruits and vegetables or becoming vegetarian.
7. They take vitamins and supplements to help support their immune system.
8. They slow down and take time to relax and fully enjoy the gift of life. Often prayer or meditation becomes a regular practice.

9. They become in tune with their body and "listen" for cues relating to energy, emotions, and body signals that are a part of daily life.
10. They rejoin with social networks and experience the joy of being of service to others. Through their own healing, they help to heal others.

This process takes dedication (intention) to work wonders, and this commitment to change will make the difference for you. When we do this type of clear, focused work, we create not only new thoughts, but also a new way of thinking. Much of what I do as a transformational agent is exactly this. I help you (1) identify the change you want to make, (2) put you in a hypnotic state where you can access your subconscious mind, (3) help you remove any blocks to your success, and (4) power-load images and suggestions that fix your success in place. When you leave my office or workshop, your job is to go home and dedicate yourself to practicing several times a day becoming a new person.

Transformative practices are multimodality in that not only do you think new thoughts, but you also feel new feelings that support the new thoughts, and you use your body, soul, and spirit to make changes. This is fascinating work, and it requires dedication and commitment.

Please don't feel overwhelmed. This is powerful stuff, and people do it all the time, so you can too! As I alluded to in the previous chapter, you have been doing this all your life. In other words, if you want to know what you believe about yourself, take a straightforward look at your life today. The Buddha once said that what we are today is the results of our thoughts yesterday. What we are going to learn to do is make this process conscious and intentional.

From Kid to Cop

From my earliest childhood, I knew I was going to be a law enforcement officer. I watched every police television show I could, from *Dragnet* and *Adam 12* to the *Adventures of the FBI*. As a teenager, I joined the Explorer Scout troop, went to the training program, wore the uniform, and then worked at the sheriff's station, doing volunteer tasks and riding along in their patrol cars. When I was seventeen, I joined the army and became a military policeman in Germany. After I was discharged from the military, I went to college and took police science courses until I was eligible to take the admissions exam to the sheriff's department. The day finally came when I took the law enforcement oath and donned the uniform of a deputy sheriff.

For ten years, I held the image in my mind of being a deputy sheriff. I used to sit in my college classes daydreaming about what it would be like to drive my patrol car with the lights and sirens blaring, and I would feel an adrenaline rush just thinking about it. I used to go to the sheriff's substations and take in all the sights and sounds. I even used my olfactory memory to "smell" gunpowder and the disinfectant that they used to clean the jail floors. In other words, I used every faculty of my mind to *become* a deputy. When the day of my oath came, it felt like the most natural thing in the world.

The change you want to make in your life need not take ten years to come to pass. I've made profound changes since then in much shorter periods, but the process has always been the same. The change I want becomes the most important idea in my mind, and I hold it to the exclusion of all evidence to the contrary.

Joseph Murphy taught that the true meaning of faith is believing that our goals have already become a reality, even though our five senses tell us differently. So, while I'm asking you to make a profound commitment to change, I want to assure you that you'll love the journey on the way to success because you'll already be living in the experience of it.

Let's Launch the New You

In some ways, this transformative process, like running a marathon, is very simple but filled with challenges and opportunities along the way. The easy part of the marathon is that all you have to do is put one foot in front of the other for twenty-six miles to complete the race. The challenges come in the form of the getting in shape to do the run, learning how to take in the exact proportions of hydration and nutrition to complete it, and sustaining the intention to see the race to the end, regardless of how long it takes you to get to the finish line.

To become a new person who is successful, prosperous, healthy, or happy is simple. You think about yourself in a new way, use your neurology to support your change, and remove anything that blocks you reaching the finish line. Your challenges are to release deeply conditioned thought patterns in your subconscious that inhibit change and to replace them with a brand-new way of being you.

Identify the Change You Want to Make: What Is Your Heart's Desire Right Now?

Is it to lose weight, break free from an addiction, substantially increase your income, launch a new career, or heal yourself from a debilitating physical condition? Using the gift of clarity, write out the thing in your life that you are going to change or create.

Example, "I want to become a successful actor in television and movies."

_____

_____

_____

_____

Write down every reason for making the change that you can think of.

Don't just think about these results; feel them in your body.

Example: "I want to become a successful actor because it will give me fame, security, and a sense of accomplishment that I crave. I want to feel the rush of accomplishment as I see my name as the credits roll, and I want to be able to buy my mother a place of her own for her golden years."

_____

_____

_____

_____

What has kept you from reaching your goal so far?

List roadblocks, feelings, emotional patterns—anything you can point to as an obstacle.

Example: "Try as I might, I can't seem to remember my lines when I go in for auditions, and I freeze up. For as long as I can remember, my family has ridiculed me for wanting to be a star. I'm so out of shape that no casting director takes me seriously. I work so many part-time jobs just to survive that I can't take any acting classes to perfect my craft."

_____

_____

_____

_____

Is your current challenge or goal the only time you've struggled to make powerful change in your life?

Look for patterns, and see what motivations are behind them.

Example: "I never did well in school because I have trouble remembering things. When I tried out for the football team but was cut after the first practice, my family laughed at me. My teachers all said I wouldn't amount to anything."

_____

_____

_____

_____

Write down again what it will feel like when you accomplish your goal.

This seems repetitive, but from here on out, we are going to focus only on your positive good. You've analyzed the problem, and now we switch into the language and neurology of the solution.

Example: "I will feel so good because I've always known that I could be a success. I will feel appreciated for my talent and hard work. I will be accepted by a whole new group of friends and will find the love of my life. I will be happy, confident, and unafraid in taking on new things and in loving my work."

_____

_____

_____

_____

The Transformative Moment

If you were in my office or in my workshop, I would lead you through a meditation and visualization like what you'll experience here. We would record it as a download, and you'd listen to it at home as you did your TW (transformational work). Get a voice recorder, and make this meditation in your own voice. If you're listening via audiobook, you've got a head start.

Before you start, make sure you are in a comfortable place where you won't be interrupted. Turn off you cell phone, landline, pager, or any other device that may interrupt you by making noise. As far as possible, make sure the temperature in the room is comfortable so you aren't distracted by heat or cold.

Pick a comfortable chair that you will always come back to as *the place* where you do your TW. If you consistently use the same place, your subconscious gets habituated to it and knows it's time to get serious about change. Obviously, there are other times and places where you'll want to do your TW, but for this introduction, make sure everything favors success.

Turn your recorder on now.

Transformative Meditation

Begin this meditation by sitting comfortably in your seat. Pick a spot on the wall in front of you, and fix your gaze there as you become aware of the breath flowing in and out of your nose.

As much as you are able, look at your spot on the wall, and become aware of my voice as I lead you through this meditation.

With your gaze on the spot on the wall, begin a three-count breath cycle—that is, gently breathe in for the count of three, hold it for the count of three, and exhale for the count of three. Do it again, breathing in for the count of three, holding it for the count of three, and exhaling for the count of three.

Your vision may get a little blurry, but keep looking at your focus point as you breathe in for the count of three, hold it for the count of three, and exhale for the count of three.

Again, looking at your spot, breathe in for the count of three, hold it for the count of three, and exhale for the count of three. As we do this work together, let my voice be the only sound that you pay attention to; any other sound becomes like white noise, leading you back to my voice.

Again, breathe in for the count of three, hold it for the count of three, and exhale for the count of three. This time, as you exhale, let your eyes gently close.

Allow your breath to return to a gentle and natural rhythm. Now your focus is on the breath at your nose and on my voice.

Since, the creative power to make change begins from a place of deep relaxation, I invite you to visualize or imagine that a gentle, beautiful light settles on the crown of your head. As it does, allow your head to begin to relax.

As the light gently moves down your head across your forehead, your ears, your eyes, your jaws, and your lips, imagine that all the muscles in your head begin to relax.

Continuing your breath at the nose and being aware of only my voice, all the light of relaxation descends to your neck and throat. Imagine that all the muscles of your neck and throat relax as your breath gets even steadier and rhythmic.

Now the light of relaxation rests on your shoulders and cascades across your arms, past your biceps and triceps, down from your elbows to your forearms and hands. You may feel a tingling in your hands as the deep relaxation that you are entering causes a change in blood flow. If you don't, that's fine as well. You are doing wonderfully.

As you continue to focus on your breath and my voice, imagine that the relaxing light embraces your chest and upper back. As it moves down to your stomach and lower back, visualize that all your muscles are relaxing, as if you have just stepped into a warm, relaxing bath.

Still breathing gently through your nose, imagine that the light makes its way down across your buttocks and genitals, down across your hips and upper legs. Feel those powerful muscles begin to relax.

Now the light continues its journey down and bathes your shins and calves in deep relaxation. And finally, it settles on your feet, as your toes relax, your instep relaxes, your ankles relax, and your feet relax.

As you continue your gentle breath, you remain aware of my voice, as you now become conscious of the space around your body. You've felt your body relax, but now see if you can feel the space between your thumbs and your fingers.

Can you feel the space on your face between your eyes? Feel the space between the other parts of your face. Take a moment to scan your body, and in so doing, discover space that you didn't know was there.

Continuing to breathe gentle in and out of your nose, and allowing my voice to be your guide, imagine that you can feel all the air around your body as a protective shell. Feel the air on your hands and arms, on your face and head, and even as you can on your legs and feet.

Spaciousness and peace are essential parts of the creative process, so as you continue to relax deeply, use your powerful imagination and feel the space around you.

Now, enjoying the breath at your nose and becoming accustomed to my voice, imagine that you are standing at the top of a beautiful wooden staircase. This staircase is strong and sturdy. It is polished to a wondrous luster. As you look at it, you notice a solid handrail on the left side of the staircase.

In a moment, I'm going to invite you to walk down the staircase, but first notice that next to the top step is a full-length, ornately decorated mirror. Look at yourself in mirror, and see yourself as you perceive yourself to be today. Maybe you feel discouraged about life, and that reflects in the mirror, or maybe you smell the odor of cigarette smoke wafting off you as you look in the mirror. Maybe you see a poor person or a lonely person or a sick person looking back at you through the mirror.

Gently acknowledge the presence of your reflection in the mirror, and give it thanks, for it has got you to this point where you are making all things new. There is no need to be angry at or ashamed of what you see in the mirror. Just acknowledge that it got you here.

Now turn and walk away from the mirror, and as you continue to breathe gently through your nose, imagine that you take hold of the handrail with your left hand. Using your left foot, step onto the first step. Then in a natural rhythm, descend the staircase, counting your steps along the way. 19, 18, 17, 16, 15, 14, 13, 12, and 11.

When you get to step number 10, pause for a moment and look down toward your destination. You notice a being standing down there, and it is so radiant that it draws you to it like a magnet. So, continue your journey down the staircase: 9, 8, 7, 6, 5, 4, 3, 2, 1, and step onto the solid ground.

Continuing to be aware of your breath as you approach the luminous being who has been waiting for your arrival. As you get closer, you notice that this being is you. This being projects confidence, health, prosperity, and love. Notice the aura that surrounds this being and that you are welcomed with open arms. Allow the being to embrace you, and imagine and feel that you are absorbed into its light and love.

In the embrace of this love, all pain and fear and sorrow to drop away. Just for this moment, you feel what it would be like to live out of the energy of your true self. And you know that this being is your future being realized now.

Your wonderful self asks what you want to accomplish in your work of transformation. Tell it now.

The being walks you to a comfortable and safe place that reminds you of your favorite place on earth. It might be a nature landscape or a favorite room or a place that you enjoyed as a child. As you find a place to sit comfortably, notice that this luminous being takes its place right behind you.

The being speaks the following words to you: "I want you to concentrate fully on what you want to accomplish now." As you begin to focus, this being puts its hands on the top of your head, and you feel a pulsating energy entering your brain as it begins to shimmer with light.

The being now says, "Imagine your desire coming true. Picture it fully and completely. What will you look like when you reach your goal? Imagine the day when you realize you've made the change you wanted to make.

"Feel the positive, strong, and wonderful feelings that become alive for you in this moment. Feel energy of success, self-appreciation, energy, vitality, joy, and pleasure coursing through your body.

"See you radiating with success as you achieve your goal. Allow the colors to go from normal to radiant. Let light sparkle all around you.

"See people congratulating you for your accomplishments. Hear their words of praise, and soak in love and goodwill. Feel happiness coursing through your body as you see your success before you.

"Now introduce the power of gratitude into your feelings. Feel successful for accomplishing the change that you desire and gratitude for the change happening to you now. Alternate between the feelings of success, healing, and accomplishment, and supercharge them with gratitude.

"Allow this process to continue for a while. Visualize your success, then feel your success. Also feel gratitude for your success. Visualize your success, then feel your success, and feel gratitude for your success.

"See the people you love jumping up and down with joy for you and your success. Feel their love coming at you as an avalanche of incredible energy. Feel grateful that you have this moment of success to share.

"Visualize your success, then feel your success, and feel gratitude for your success. Visualize your success, then feel your success, and feel gratitude for your success."

Your luminous guide behind you continues to pour strength and love and energy into you as you visualize your success, then feel your success, and feel gratitude for your success.

Now gently allow all the images to drop from sight, and imagine only that you are being bathed in the light of success and love. But allow those supercharged feelings of success to continue to echo through your being.

Feel the love, feel the satisfaction, feel the success, feel the healing, feel the energy, feel the flexibility, feel the joy. And then bathe all those feelings in gratitude. Allow thankfulness to mingle with your feelings of success and burst into an explosion of light, joy, and love more powerful than the world has ever seen.

If another feeling or memory arises and tries to take you out of your super state, recognize that it is just energy passing through. Let it drift away. Then return to your visual imagery of you standing on the stage of your success. As you do this, feel your powerful, positive emotions return, and wrap them all in gratitude. Visualize your success, then feel your success, and feel gratitude for your success.

When the feelings of success and gratitude are strong again, let the images drop from your mind, and sit there bathed in light and your life-changing feelings.

You notice your guide's hands are now on your shoulders, and you feel your guide bend down and whisper into your ear, "The future is now; you *are* the dream come true, you *are* success, you *are* health, you are prosperity, and you *are* joy. The old things have passed away, and all things are made new.

"Imagine and feel what it is like living in the solution, in the place of creation and manifestation now. If money is your goal, *know* that your bank accounts are full and working for you; if professional success was your goal *know* that your advancement has arrived; if healing is your goal, *know* that your body is strong, and healthy and true."

Know that the future is now, and feel what it's like to live in the solution with gratitude and joy.

So, with a heart filled with gratitude, you stand before your guide, that radiant expression of yourself, who says, "From this point on, all heaven and earth is ordered to your success.

"Trust that when a decision is to be made that your subconscious mind will provide the best answer. Know that when a personal or professional connection needs to be made, the Divine will order such a meeting at just the right time. And remember that all the resources you need—spiritual, mental or material—are now at the service of your success."

Feeling love, joy, peace, exhilaration, and gratitude, rest for a moment in all the wonder of the new you as you return to the present moment, to the chair in which you sit, in the room where your miracle has begun.

With a couple of delicious cleansing breaths, open your eyes and sit in a state of wonder. Allow all the positive, powerful feelings of accomplishment to resonate through you like an echo in huge cave.

Turn the recorder off.

Please Remember ...

By now you know that these feelings are your goal. By linking your powerful imagination with strong, positive emotion, your subconscious "gets the message" and establishes what I call the new normal. When you feel lost or disoriented, briefly flash back to the panorama of your success. Allow those positive, life-changing feelings to arrive, and allow them to become your new default. Use the integration of your imagination, powerful feelings, and new knowing to keep you focused on living as the successful person that you are. The outer world will catch up in short order.

Remember the agreement we made based on the gift of your intention: you will do whatever it takes to birth the new you. Starting right now, do this meditation at least twice a day for twenty minutes at each sitting. At first it may seem exciting, and then it may seem like a chore, but keep at it because you are writing a new script for your life, and it takes as much repetition and reinforcement as it did to write the old one.

When asked about how he could create such masterpieces of art, Michelangelo answered, "The best artist has that thought alone which is contained within the marble shell; the sculptor's hand can only break the spell, to free the figures slumbering in the stone." Your life is your masterpiece waiting to be revealed from within the stone of your mind. Let's work together to bring it forth.

Summary

This chapter guided you on a transformative journey. We've seen that the goal is not merely to change a habit, but to change our very lives. We are capable of so much more in our lives, and we can learn to accelerate our growth and development by walking the transformational journey.

To become a new person is to think new thoughts, to feel new feelings, and to become a master at using our neurology to effect and support our changes. By experiencing the meditation of transformation in this chapter, we've seen how using relaxation and visualization, and enhancing our feeling state, we can introduce change at the subconscious level. Then, with continued and dedicated practice, we can make the change we desire and the people we want to be as our new default. By doing this, we create a larger sense of our self, and we recognize that we are coming home to the Divine's vision of us from the beginning.

CHAPTER 8

CLOSING THOUGHTS

I hope this introduction to the power of your magnificent mind has been informative and transformative. We have just scratched the surface,[3] and as you undertake your program of change, you will have the opportunity to learn something new every day. As you more fully integrate your conscious and subconscious minds, learn about emotional states that support or block your process, and practice transformation, you will be amazed at your progress.

Your family, friends, and colleagues will notice something different about your attitudes and achievements. People will notice your heightened sense of positivity, clarity, and inspiration. You will become magnetic to others, and they will want what you have. Your physical and emotional health will become vibrant, and you will exude a humble confidence that you didn't know was possible.

Once you've mastered your magnificent mind, the options for your success will reveal themselves in incredible ways. You might have an intuitive flash to make a call to a client that results in a profitable business arrangement. A phone call from a long-lost friend might lead

---

[3] We didn't spend much time on the wonder of epigenetics, the body's ability to change gene structure and function, or on the power of brain wave technology in making change. In my workshops, we do dive into these crucial understandings.

to a new job offer for you. A potent dream gives you the answer to a problem that has challenged you for years. Physical abilities begin to return to your body, and you experience vibrancy and health that you thought were long gone. Or you might notice that you can "read" people more easily and connect with them in a powerful way. These are but a few of the benefits of learning how to become a master of transformation.

Another profound benefit of using your mind in the way that it was created is that you'll have a heightened sense of spirituality and inspiration, if you so desire. In writing this book, I haven't talked much about spirituality for a reason. In my opinion, we are living in a time when the state of religion is undergoing a powerful shift— and as you know, any discussion of religion can be polarizing and counterproductive. In my generation, however, the study of the spiritual life and our connection to transcendence is becoming disconnected from traditional religious practice. You can see this in the proliferation of all kinds of yoga practices, the embrace of Eastern spiritual and philosophical traditions, mythopoetic dream work, and a return to earth-centered rituals. Even in some of traditional religious practice there is a move away from dogmatism toward embracing a contemplative or mystical form of spirituality.

We cannot conclude our study of the mind without understanding that the subconscious is our doorway to Divinity. Since symbols and images are the language of the subconscious, this opens the door to deeper connections within ourselves of what some call the higher self, the actualized self, or simply God.

One author suggested that the Middle Ages in Europe was the age of the subconscious mind, as people lived and breathed symbolism and mythic story. Only in the post-enlightenment has the conscious mind developed, and our subconscious connection to the inner world seemed to grow dormant. But currently we are seeing a yearning again for the meaning that symbolic and transcendent experiences provide—and for this we can thank the return to our subconscious minds.

I've worked with people long enough to know that as they deepen their understanding of and contact with their mind, they experience a spiritual impulse to *be more, love more, and give more.* And if that isn't the definition of a healthy spirituality, it will do until one comes along. So, if you've not been a particularly "spiritual" person, don't be surprised if a yearning to experience life in all its abundance takes hold of you. Some people find that religious expression becomes important for them; others come to deeply appreciate the beauty of nature, music, and the arts; still others find a way through meditation and similar practices to deepen their connection with the greater world—and all of this comes from discovering your magnificent mind.

The Gift of Gratitude

During your transformative meditation (which you are doing at least twice a day), you will notice that special attention was paid to experiencing a state of gratitude for the positive feelings and changes that are taking place in your life. We know that when people intentionally feel gratitude, they can make positive changes more quickly. This should make perfect sense to you now, as you understand the link between your mind, body, and emotions.

Dartmouth University has done research into the way that gratitude changes your physical and mental well-being. In their work on the connection between gratitude and wholeness, Martin Seligman, Robert Emmons, and Michael McCullough have discovered that people who keep gratitude journals on a weekly basis have been found to exercise more regularly, have fewer physical symptoms, feel better about their lives, and feel more optimistic about their upcoming week as compared to those who keep journals recording the stressors or neutral events of their lives.

Brain expert Dr. Daniel Amen studied the function of gratitude on the brain and discovered that the brain of a person who practices gratitude functions differently from that of a person who doesn't. In these tests, he discovered that when subjects were asked to think about something that they were grateful for, the frontal lobes of the brain experienced a significant increase in blood flow and electrical activity. In subjects who were asked to think of things they were resentful for or hated in their lives, they showed a reduction in blood flow and electricity to those same frontal lobes. The frontal lobes are part of our "executive functioning," where decisions are made, so it stands to reason that a more vibrant and active frontal lobe will result in you making decisions that serve your success.

So, by practicing gratitude, both during your transformative meditations and throughout the rest of your day, you change your blood chemistry and put your best self to work for you. Addictions and recovery expert Melody Beattie once wrote that gratitude "unlocks the fullness of life. It turns what we have into enough, and more. It turns denial into acceptance, chaos to order, confusion to clarity. It can turn a meal into a feast, a house into a home, a stranger into a friend." Now we know why. Gratitude connects the conscious and subconscious mind in a powerful way, and the miraculous begins to unfold.

I end this book filled with gratitude. I am grateful for my work with people, and I'm glad to extend my reach through these pages to touch you as well. Being a transformational agent is one of the deepest joys of my life, as I get to see people become happier, fulfilled, healed, connected, and successful. I am grateful that, in reading this book, you have planted seeds in your subconscious mind that will reap an abundant harvest as you make all this real in your life.

Our next step is to work together. Whether it is in my offices in Beverly Hills, at your home or office around the world, at a conference, or by Skype, I think it's time that we connect and take the next step in your journey of success, fulfillment, health, and joy. See you soon—and remember, do your homework, become the new you, and stay grateful!

To continue your transformative journey with Dr. David James, please use email him at davidjameshypnosis.com or call his main Beverly Hills office at (818) 724-9314. Subscribe to David's website at www.davidjameshypnosis.com *for updates and further opportunities to connect and grow.*

APPENDIX

RECOMMENDED READING

I am indebted to the following masters of transformation and the wisdom I discovered in the pages of their books. The marketplace is full of wonderful teachers and resources, but these are the ones who contributed to the writing of this book.

Daniel Amen

Change Your Brain, Change Your Life: The Breakthrough Program for Conquering Anxiety, Depression, Obsessiveness, Anger, and Impulsiveness.
Three Rivers Press, 1999

Gregg Braden

The Spontaneous Healing of Belief: Shattering the Paradigm of False Limits
Hay House Publications, 2008

Joe Dispenza

Breaking the Habit of Being Yourself: How to lose your mind and create a new one.
Hay House Publications, 2011

You Are the Placebo: Making Your Mind Matter
Hay House Publications, 2014

Sunny Sea Gold

*Food: The Good Girl's Drug: How to Stop
Using Food to Control Your Feelings*
Berkeley Press, 2011

Napoleon Hill

Think and Grow Rich
Tarcher Press, 2005

Harish Malhorta

*Metaphors of Healing: Playful Language in
Psychotherapy and Everyday Life*
Hamilton Books, 2014

John G. Kappas

Professional Hypnotism Manual: A Practical Approach for Modern Times
Panorama Publishing, 2009

Lester Levenson

*Keys to the Ultimate Freedom: Thoughts and
Talks on Personal Transformation*
The Sedona Institute, 1993

Bruce Lipton

The Biology of Belief: Unleashing the Power of
Consciousness, Matter and Miracles
Hay House Publications, 2008

Joseph Murphy

The Power of your Subconscious Mind
SoHo Books, 2103

Think Yourself Rich
Prentice Hall Press, 1972

ABOUT THE AUTHOR

Dr. David James practices hypnotherapy and psychotherapy in Beverly Hills, California, as part of the New Visions Medical Group. He is the author of two previous books on the spiritual life of men and has written articles for journals and magazines on the intersection of psychology and spirituality.

He holds a PhD in clinical psychology and graduate degrees in theology and spirituality. As an expert in personal transformation, he is an in-demand speaker and retreat leader.

Dr. James was a professor of psychology and spirituality at the Trinity College of Graduate Studies in Anaheim, California, and speaks in professional forums across the United States and in Canada.

He began his professional career as a deputy with the Los Angeles County Sheriff's Department and retired from the Chino Police Department as a sergeant. As a police officer, he worked in the Patrol Division, Crime-Scene Investigations Bureau, Detective Bureau, and Community Relations Detail.

He has been a consultant, trainer, retreat director, and counselor in faith-based settings and served as a priest and pastor in Episcopal congregations in California and Washington.

Dr. James is a frequent guest on radio and television programs as he shares the profound transformation that is possible by using the power of the mind.